MS-DOS
Explain

D0476919

ALSO AVAILABLE

MS-DOS 6
Explained

by

N. Kantaris
and
P.R.M. Oliver

BERNARD BABANI (publishing) LTD.
THE GRAMPIANS
SHEPHERDS BUSH ROAD
LONDON W6 7NF
ENGLAND

PLEASE NOTE

© 1993 BERNARD BABANI (publishing) LTD

First Published – December 1993
Reprinted – June 1994
Reprinted – June 1995

British Library Cataloguing in Publication Data:

Kantaris N.
  MS-DOS 6 Explained
  I. Title II. Oliver, P.R.M.
  005.4

  ISBN 0 85934 341 3

Printed and Bound in Great Britain by Cox & Wyman Ltd, Reading

ABOUT THIS BOOK

MS-DOS 6 Explained has been written for those who want to get to grips with MS-DOS in the fastest possible time. No previous knowledge of the operating system is assumed, but the book does not describe how to set up your computer hardware, or how to install Microsoft Windows. If you need to know more about the latter topic, then may we suggest that you also refer to the book *A Concise User's Guide to Windows 3.1* (BP325), also published by BERNARD BABANI (publishing) Ltd.

This book does not seek to replace the documentation you receive with MS-DOS 6, but only to supplement and explain it. Apart from the basics, the book also deals with the enhancements to be found in both versions 6.0 and 6.2 of MS-DOS, several aspect of which are new. There is, for example, the addition of a number of new commands, but more importantly is the inclusion of several disc utilities, such as the DoubleSpace program which can double the capacity of your hard disc at no extra cost, the DoubleGuard program (new to version 6.2) which tests the integrity of the DoubleSpace data, the Scan Disk program (new to version 6.2) which detects and repairs errors on your hard disc whether compressed or uncompressed, the MemMaker program which configures your system automatically to give you maximum conventional memory, and the Anti-Virus program which detects and removes computer viruses.

This book was written with the busy person in mind. It is not necessary to read several hundred pages covering all there is to know about a subject, when a few selected pages can do the same thing quite adequately! Naturally, selectivity of subject matter is of paramount importance, so that the reader does not miss vital points. In particular, the book seeks to bring to the forefront and exploit the inherent simplicity in the MS-DOS operating system by presenting, with examples, the principles of what you need to know, when you need to know it.

At the same time, the book has been written in such a way as to also act as a reference guide, long after you have mastered most MS-DOS commands. To this end, a summary of the commands supported by the MS-DOS operating system is given in the penultimate section of the book. The commands are explained with relevant examples and, as such, the section can serve as a quick reference guide..

With the help of this book, it is hoped that you will be able to get the most out of your computer in terms of efficiency, productivity and enjoyment, and that you will be able to do it in the shortest, most effective and informative way.

If you would like to purchase a floppy disc containing all the files/programs which appear in this, or any other listed book(s) by the same author(s), then fill-in the form at the back of the book and send it to P. R. M. Oliver at the stipulated address.

ABOUT THE AUTHORS

Noel Kantaris graduated in Electrical Engineering at Bristol University and after spending three years in the Electronics Industry in London, took up a Tutorship in Physics at the University of Queensland. Research interests in Ionospheric Physics, led to the degrees of M.E. in Electronics and Ph.D. in Physics. On return to the UK, he took up a Post-Doctoral Research Fellowship in Radio Physics at the University of Leicester, and in 1973 a Senior Lectureship in Engineering at Camborne School of Mines, Cornwall, where since 1978 he has also assumed the responsibility of Head of Computing.

Phil Oliver graduated in Mining Engineering at Camborne School of Mines in 1967 and since then has specialised in most aspects of surface mining technology, with a particular emphasis on computer related techniques. He has worked in Guyana, Canada, several Middle Eastern countries, South Africa and the United Kingdom, on such diverse projects as: the planning and management of bauxite, iron, gold and coal mines; rock excavation contracting in the U.K.; international mining equipment sales and technical back up; international mine consulting for a major mining house in South Africa. In 1988 he took up a Senior Lectureship at Camborne School of Mines in Surface Mining and Management.

ACKNOWLEDGEMENTS

We would like to thank colleagues at the Camborne School of Mines for the helpful tips and suggestions which assisted us in the writing of this book.

TRADEMARKS

CONTENTS

1. MS-DOS OVERVIEW

Most 16-bit microcomputers use Microsoft's Disc Operating System (MS-DOS) as the prime means of interaction between user and computer. Owners of IBM PCs know this operating system as PC-DOS, which is IBM's implementation of MS-DOS. The name MS-DOS or DOS will be used throughout this book to distinguish this operating system from another popular one, namely Digital Research's DR-DOS.

Versions of MS-DOS

Since its inception in 1981, MS-DOS has been the standard operating system for personal computers and by now is being used by more than 50 million people. As the number of users increased over the years, so too has the complexity of applications run on their PCs. To meet these ever increasing demands, MS-DOS has also increased its functionality several times in the form of *new* versions, as shown in the table below.

Version	Date	Main changes in functionality
1.0	1981	Microsoft renames to MS-DOS the Original Disc Operating System 86-QDOS written by Seattle Computer Products. IBM calls this PC-DOS.
1.25	1982	Provides support for double-sided discs and fixes a number of bugs. IBM calls this PC-DOS 1.1
2.0	1983	Provides support for a 10MB hard disc, subdirectories, and 360KB floppy discs.
2.11	1983	Provides support for extended character set.
3.0	1984	Provides support for 1.2MB floppy disc and larger capacity hard disc (up to 32MB).
3.1	1984	Provides support for PC networks.

3.3	1987	Provides support for PS/2 computer range, 1.44MB, 3½" floppy discs, partitioning of hard discs, and a number of additional codepages.
4.0	1988	Provides support for extended memory (EMS), hard disc partitions beyond 32MB (up to 2GB), and the graphical user interface DOS shell.
4.01	1989	Fix bugs in 4.0 version.
5.0	1991	Adds the ability to run DOS in high memory and certain device drivers in upper memory. Adopts a full screen editor and context sensitive help, and supports the 2.88MB floppy disc.
6.0	1993	Includes Double Space, Anti-Virus, and Defragmenter disc utilities. Adds the Move & Deltree commands and a new MSBACKUP utility. Provides for multiple start-up configurations.
6.2	1993	Includes DoubleGuard to protect memory used by Double Space, which can now be uninstalled. Supports a one-pass DISKCOPY, CD-ROM caching and replaces the CHKDSK command with SCANDISK.

The Structure of MS-DOS

To understand how to use MS-DOS you must understand its underlying structure. The various DOS administrative functions are contained in three separate main files (later on we will explain what files mean and their naming convention). These are:

MSDOS.SYS
IO.SYS
COMMAND.COM

or IBMDOS.COM, IBMBIO.COM and COMMAND.COM, in the case of the IBM PC.

The first file is the core of the operating system, while the second one, also called the Basic Input Output System (BIOS), allows the core to communicate with the hardware. It is the BIOS that is adapted by manufacturers of different hardware so that the operating system can appear to function in the same way, even though there might be differences in hardware design. The last file, COMMAND.COM, is the Command Processor which analyses what is typed at the keyboard, and if correct, finds and starts execution of the appropriate command.

MS-DOS has over forty built-in commands, normally referred to as 'internal commands', instantly available to the user as they reside in memory. In addition to these internal commands, there are over ninety 'external' commands which are to be found on the MS-DOS distribution discs. The machine program which makes up each of these external commands is saved in a *file* under an appropriate name with a .COM or .EXE extension to the filename (more about this later). Collectively, these internal and external commands make up the computer's Disc Operating System (DOS). These commands will be examined in detail in the following chapters of this book.

Booting up the System:

Whenever you start your computer by switching on the power, the system is booted up, which is normally indicated by the appearance of a C> or A> prompt, for booting from a hard or floppy disc drive, respectively. The word 'normally' was used here because you might be running the DOS Shell (or some other interface), in which case you will not see the usual C> prompt.

Now, displaying a listing of the directory (by typing **DIR** at the prompt and pressing <Enter>), will reveal the contents of your disc, but neither of the first two System files (MSDOS.SYS and IO.SYS) will appear on the directory list as they are hidden. Only the third file (COMMAND.COM) will be displayed.

In addition to these three special files, there are a number of other DOS files which perform various important tasks.

3

These are collectively known as the DOS utilities and will be examined in detail later. To be able to distinguish between disc drives, MS-DOS refers to them by a letter followed by a colon, i.e. C: or A: for the prime drive of the appropriate system. In a twin floppy disc-based system, there are two drives; A: and B:, with drive A: being the leftmost or uppermost of the two, while on a hard disc-based system there is a hard disc drive, C: (additional ones are named D:, E:, and so on) and a floppy disc drive, A: (with one possible extra, named B:). DOS allows you to also refer to drive A: as drive B:, so that you can copy files from one floppy disc to another using a single floppy disc drive. Users on networked systems can access a network hard disc by assigning it as another drive on their micro, namely as E: or Z:

On booting up a microcomputer, the following tasks are performed:

- A self test on its Random Access Memory (RAM) is performed.

- A check is made to see if a floppy disc is in drive A:, and if there is, whether it is a System disc. If it is, it boots the system from the A: drive.

- If no floppy exists in drive A:, an attempt is made to boot the system from drive C:, if there is one, otherwise in the case of the IBM, it goes into Read Only Memory (ROM) based BASIC.

- Configures the system by executing the CONFIG.SYS file.

- Reads the BIOS and the MS-DOS operating system.

- Loads into RAM the COMMAND.COM file so that internal commands can be made available instantly.

- Executes the commands within the AUTOEXEC.BAT file, if one exists, otherwise it asks for the Date and Time which can be reset at this point. Pressing the <Enter> key, confirms what is displayed.

Should you receive any error message while these tasks are being performed, you could restart the process, after rectifying the error, by pressing simultaneously the three keys marked **Ctrl**, **Alt** and **Del**, shown in this book as **<Ctrl+Alt+Del>**. This will re-boot the system, and is referred to as a 'warm re-boot'. In contrast, re-booting the system by either switching the power off and then back on again or pressing the 'Reset' button, is referred to as a 'cold re-boot'.

Internal DOS Commands

MS-DOS has nearly forty internal commands built into it which are instantly available as they reside in memory. These are listed on the following couple of page.

Command	Meaning
BREAK	Sets the Ctrl+Break check on or off. Used either at the command prompt or in the CONFIG.SYS file.
BUFFERS	Allocates memory for a specified number of disc buffers from within your CONFIG.SYS file.
CALL	Calls one batch file from another without exiting from the first one.
CD or CHDIR	Changes the current directory.
CHCP	Displays or changes the active code page.
CLS	Clears the screen.
COPY	Copies files.
CTTY	Changes the standard Input/Output device.
DATE	Displays or sets the system date.
DEL	Deletes the specified files.
DEVICE	Loads a specified device driver into memory from within your CONFIG.SYS file.
DIR	Displays the disc directory.
DOS	Specifies from within your CONFIG.SYS file that DOS should maintain a link to the upper memory area, load part of itself into high memory area (HMA), or both.
ECHO	Sets Echo to on or off.
ERASE	See DEL command.

EXIT	Exits to the previous command level.
FCBS	Specifies from within your CONFIG.SYS file the number of File Control Blocks (FCBs) that DOS can have open at the same time.
FILES	Specifies from within your CONFIG.SYS file the number of files that DOS can access at one time.
FOR	Repeats a command for each item in a set.
GOTO	Jumps to a labelled line within the same batch file.
IF	Allows conditional execution of commands within a batch file.
INCLUDE	Includes from within your CONFIG.SYS file the contents of one configuration block within another.
INSTALL	Loads from within your CONFIG.SYS file a memory-resident program into memory.
LASTDRIVE	Specifies from within your CONFIG.SYS file the maximum number of drives you can access.
LH (LOADHIGH)	Loads a program into upper memory.
MD or MKDIR	Makes (creates) a new directory.
NUMLOCK	Specifies from within your CONFIG.SYS file whether the NUMLOCK key is set ON or OFF.
PATH	Searches alternative directories.
PAUSE	Pauses execution of the batch file.
PROMPT	Changes the system prompt.
RD or RMDIR	Removes (deletes) a directory.
REM	Allows remarks to be added in a batch file.
REN or RENAME	Renames files.
SET	Changes the system parameters.
SHELL	Specifies from within CONFIG.SYS the location of the command interpreter you want DOS to use.
SHIFT	Allows more than 10 replaceable parameters in a batch file.

STACKS	Supports the dynamic use of data stacks to handle hardware interrupts. This command can only be used from within your CONFIG.SYS file.
SUBMENU	Defines from within CONFIG.SYS an item on a start-up menu that, when selected, displays another set of options.
SWITCHES	Specifies from within CONFIG.SYS special DOS options.
TIME	Displays or sets the system time.
TYPE	Displays a specified text file.
VER	Displays the MS-DOS version.
VERIFY	Checks disc writing.
VOL	Displays the disc volume label.

The internal DOS commands (most of which will be explained later), together with the rest of the operating system, occupy some 65 KB of RAM, as they are loaded into memory on booting up the system. Where exactly in memory these commands are loaded, depends on the version of DOS being used and the type of processor in your system.

For example, if you were using an MS-DOS version prior to version 5, then all the DOS commands would load in 'conventional' memory, which is the first 640 KB of memory in your computer. If you are using MS-DOS version 5 or 6, in a computer with Intel's 80286 or higher processor, part of the DOS commands could be loaded into 'extended' memory (the memory between 1 and 16 MB - or even higher on 80386 and 80486 machines), freeing at least 45 KB of 'conventional' memory for your DOS applications.

Illustrating Internal MS-DOS Commands

As an illustration of internal MS-DOS commands, consider the two which allow you to re-set the date and time of your computer's clock. If you are running the DOS Shell (not shipped with MS-DOS 6.2), it will be necessary to select the 'Command Prompt' option from the Main menu at the lower half of the DOS Shell screen, in order to emulate what is presented on the next page.

The DATE & TIME Commands:

Your computer is equipped with an internal clock, whose date and time can be changed. Typing the command

DATE

at the C> prompt, evokes the response

```
Current date is dd/mm/yy
Enter new date:
```

You can either type a new date, or press <Enter> to indicate no change. The above date format assumes that you have included the command COUNTRY=xxx, where xxx is a three digit code representing your country, in your CONFIG.SYS file (to be discussed later), otherwise the date will be shown in mm/dd/yy format. Similarly, typing the command

TIME

at the C> prompt, evokes the response

```
Current time is Hrs:Mins:Secs
Enter new time:
```

at which point you can either type a new time, or press <Enter> to indicate that time is not to be changed.

External DOS Commands

DOS provides over a hundred additional commands which, to avoid eating up more of the computer's memory, reside on disc. These are known as external commands and can only be invoked if a disc containing the required files is accessible. In the case of a floppy disc-based system some of these files will be found on the System disc in the A: drive (DOS can be installed on floppies). For a hard disc-based system, these additional files would have been transferred onto the DOS subdirectory of the C: drive and can be accessed from it.

Files and the Disc Directory

To see a list of the DOS directory, type **DIR** at the A> prompt (for a floppy disc-based system) or type **DIR \DOS** at the C> prompt (for a hard disc-based system), and press <Enter>.

If you are running the DOS Shell, select the DOS subdirectory (by pointing and clicking with the mouse, or pressing the <Tab> key to move to the 'Directory Tree' and using the directional keys to highlight the option). If you want to type the **DIR \DOS** command, select the 'Command Prompt' option from the 'Main' menu of the DOS Shell.

Amongst the many files to be listed will be the ones shown below, the name, size and creation dates of which depend on the version of MS-DOS you are running on your computer.

Filename	Extension	Size	Date	Time
APPEND	EXE	10774	30/09/93	6:20
CHKDSK	EXE	12241	30/09/93	6:20
COMMAND	COM	54619	30/09/93	6:20
DISKCOPY	COM	13335	30/09/93	6:20
FORMAT	COM	22916	30/09/93	6:20
KEYBOARD	SYS	34598	30/09/93	6:20
LABEL	EXE	9390	10/03/93	6:00
OS2	TXT	6358	10/03/93	6:00
PRINT	EXE	15656	30/09/93	6:20
QBASIC	HLP	130881	10/03/93	6:00
RESTORE	EXE	38342	30/09/93	6:20
SCANDISK	EXE	119761	30/09/93	6:20
SORT	EXE	6938	30/09/93	6:20
XCOPY	EXE	16930	30/09/93	6:20

Note that a filename consists of up to 8 alphanumeric characters (letters and numbers only) and has a three letter extension, separated from the filename by a period, i.e. COMMAND.COM or CONFIG.SYS, without any spaces in between, unlike the listing appearing on your screen, where the periods have been omitted (but not in a DOS Shell directory listing) and the extensions have been tabulated as above.

Some of these files might have different extensions from the ones shown above, i.e. .EXE might appear as .COM in your system, as the extensions tend to differ for different versions of MS-DOS. The size of each file (in bytes) is also given on the listing together with the date and time it was created, which again might differ for different versions.

The extensions .COM, .EXE, and .SYS (which stand for 'Command', 'Executable' and 'System') are the most common extensions of the files which make up MS-DOS. They contain instructions which are executed directly by the computer. Other extensions commonly used by programs or users are:

.BAK   .BAS   .BAT   .DAT   .HLP   .TXT   .TMP

which indicate 'back-up' files, 'Basic' programs, 'batch' files, 'data' files, 'help' files, 'text' files and 'temporary' files, respectively.

Command Parameters, Switches & Filters:

Returning to the result of issuing the DIR command; what is more likely to have happened in your case (unless you are running the DOS Shell - to be discussed shortly) is that the listing of the first half of the files on your disc will have scrolled out of view. In all, there are approximately one hundred utility files on the DOS subdirectory and you can only see the last twenty or so. To stop the scrolling of a long directory, use the /P switch after the DIR command, as follows:

```
DIR \DOS /P
```

which will page the directory, displaying twenty files at a time. Alternatively, you could see all the files with the extension .COM sorted alphabetically by using the SORT filter, as follows:

```
DIR \DOS\*.COM |SORT
```

where the wildcard character '*' stands for 'all' files.

Commands can be entered in either uppercase or lower-case letters, but you must provide a space between the command and its parameters. For example, to obtain a listing of all the .EXE files on the DOS directory in paged format, you can type

```
DIR \DOS\*.EXE /P
```

or
```
dir \dos\*.exe /p
```

but you must type one space between the R (or r) of 'dir' and the back-slash (\). The space between the E (or e) and the forward slash (/) is optional; its presence only serves to improve readability.

Had you not included a space after DIR in the above command, MS-DOS would have responded with its favoured error message,

```
Bad Command or file name
```

which does not tell you very much, except that MS-DOS does not understand you!

The wildcard character '*' can also be used as part of the filename. For example,

```
DIR \DOS\DOS*.*
```

will list all the files with all extensions on the DOS directory, starting with the three characters DOS, irrespective of the ending of the filenames. There are 9 such files in MS-DOS 5 and 6.

The full MS-DOS command should also specify which drive you want to access, if it does not refer to the currently logged drive. Thus, typing

```
DIR A:DOS*.*
```

will access the specified files on the current directory of the A: drive.

A more precise wildcard is the query character '?' which can be substituted for a single character in a filename. For example, typing

```
DIR \DOS\DOS????.*
```

will list three files which happen to have only four letters following the letters DOS. The three files mentioned above exist only in versions 5 and 6 of MS-DOS.

Upgrading to MS-DOS 6

It is worth upgrading from an earlier version of MS-DOS to version 6.0 or 6.2, because of the inclusion of new and improved commands and utility programs that can improve the efficiency of your computer. MS-DOS 6 includes the following new or improved features:

- DoubleSpace, which compresses files before storing them on either your hard or floppy discs. Version 6.2 includes DoubleGuard to check data integrity.

- MemMaker, a program that optimises your computer's memory by moving device drivers and memory-resident programs into upper memory, thus freeing conventional memory so that programs can run faster and more efficiently.

- Anti-Virus, a program that identifies and removes more than one thousand known viruses from your computer system.

- Backup, a program that makes backing up your data very easy indeed.

- Undelete, an enhanced program that allows you to select one of three levels of protection in case you accidentally delete a file.

- If you choose to install the last three programs for Windows (there are options for DOS and Windows), then Setup creates a new group in Program Manager named Microsoft Tools that contains icons for each program.

- The ability to define more than one configuration for your system in your CONFIG.SYS file.

- Defragmenter, a program that reorganises files on your hard disc so they are contiguous, which minimises access time of these files.

- Help, a program that provides a complete on-line help on all MS-DOS commands.

- Interlnk, a program that allows easy transfer of files between computers.

12

Installing MS-DOS 6

Installation of MS-DOS 6 must be carried out by using the Setup program on Disc #1 of the three distribution discs. However, before starting with the installation you must prepare a floppy disc by formatting it (two if your computer uses 360KB floppy disc drives) to be used by Setup as the 'Uninstall' disc(s), in case you change your mind and you want to undo the MS-DOS 6 installation.

Further, you must make sure that you disable all Disc-Caching, Delete-Protection, and Anti-Virus programs that might be running in your system. To do so, edit your AUTOEXEC.BAT and CONFIG.SYS files by inserting a REM statement at the beginning of each line that contains the start-up commands for these programs. Next, save the edited files and restart your computer by using the **Ctrl+Alt+Del** key combination.

To run Setup, place Disc #1 in your floppy disc drive and type

    a:setup

The first Setup screen is displayed, as follows:

```
Microsoft MS-DOS 6 Setup

        Welcome to Setup.

        The Setup program prepares MS-DOS 6 to run on your
        computer.

        · To set up MS-DOS now, press ENTER.

        · To learn more about Setup before continuing, press F1.

        · To quit Setup without installing MS-DOS, press F3.




ENTER=Continue  F1=Help  F3=Exit  F5=Remove Color
```

Pressing the **F1** function key gives you information about Setup, while pressing <Enter> proceeds with the installation.

13

If you proceed with the installation, MS-DOS informs you of the need for 'Uninstall' disc(s) in the following screen:

```
Microsoft MS-DOS 6 Setup


       During Setup, you will need to provide and label one
       or two floppy disks. Each disk can be unformatted
       or newly formatted and must work in drive A. (If you
       use 360K disks, you may need two disks; otherwise,
       you need only one disk.)

       Label the disk(s) as follows:

          UNINSTALL #1
          UNINSTALL #2 (if needed)

       Setup saves some of your original DOS files on the
       UNINSTALL disk(s), and others on your hard disk in a
       directory named OLD_DOS.x. With these files, you can
       restore your original DOS if necessary.

          · When you finish labeling your UNINSTALL disk(s),
            press ENTER to continue Setup.


ENTER=Continue  F1=Help  F3=Exit
```

It is, therefore a good idea to have such disc(s) ready before you start Setup, rather than having to interrupt the program.

Next, Setup scans your computer for the system settings and asks for confirmation, as follows:

```
Microsoft MS-DOS 6 Setup


       Setup will use the following system settings:


       DOS Type:       MS-DOS
       MS-DOS Path:    C:\DOS
       Display Type:   VGA

       The settings are correct.


       If all the settings are correct, press ENTER.

       To change a setting, press the UP ARROW or DOWN ARROW key until
       the setting is selected. Then press ENTER to see alternatives.




ENTER=Continue  F1=Help  F3=Exit
```

If all the settings are correct, simply press <Enter> to go on.

14

Setup then asks you whether you would like the programs Backup, Undelete, and Anti-Virus to be installed, and offers the Windows versions of these programs as default and lists the size of these options, as follows:

```
Microsoft MS-DOS 6 Setup

       The following programs can be installed on your computer.

                      Program for               Bytes used

       Backup:        Windows only              884,736
       Undelete:      Windows only              278,528
       Anti-Virus:    Windows only              786,432

       Install the listed programs.

       Space required for MS-DOS and programs:  6,149,696
       Space available on drive C:              29,401,088



       To install the listed programs, press ENTER.  To see a list
       of available options, press the UP or DOWN ARROW key to
       highlight a program, and then press ENTER.

ENTER=Continue  F1=Help  F3=Exit
```

If you want to install the DOS version of these programs, then highlight the one required and press <Enter>. The space required on your hard disc to install these programs for both DOS and Windows, is as follows:

```
Microsoft MS-DOS 6 Setup

       The following programs can be installed on your computer.

                      Program for               Bytes used

       Backup:        Windows and MS-DOS        1,785,856
       Undelete:      Windows and MS-DOS        278,528
       Anti-Virus:    Windows and MS-DOS        1,032,192

       Install the listed programs.

       Space required for MS-DOS and programs:  7,296,576
       Space available on drive C:              29,401,088



       To install the listed programs, press ENTER.  To see a list
       of available options, press the UP or DOWN ARROW key to
       highlight a program, and then press ENTER.

ENTER=Continue  F1=Help  F3=Exit
```

After a warning message not to interrupt the installation, Setup starts to install MS-DOS 6. From this point on, the process is automatic. A few seconds after starting you are asked to insert the UNINSTALL disc into drive A: so that should you change your mind later, you can go back to your original DOS version.

During installation, several messages appear on your screen telling you how to increase your hard disc space by typing DBLSPACE at the command prompt after installation is complete, how to optimise your computer's memory (if you have a 386 or higher processor) by typing MEMMAKER at the command prompt after installation is complete, and what Anti-Virus, Backup and Undelete can do for you.

The complete installation takes about half an hour. If it is successful, the following message appears on your screen:

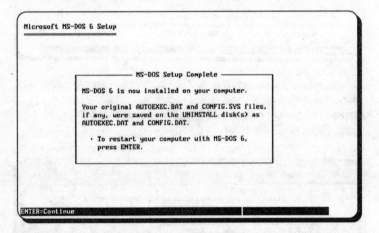

Pressing <Enter> restarts your computer with MS-DOS 6 with all the utility programs available to you so that you can look after your system more efficiently. However, before you start using any of these utilities, first refer to Chapters 5, 6 and 7.

Your old DOS files have been moved to the OLD_DOS.1 directory on your hard disc. These files and the information contained in your 'Uninstall' disc are required should you ever decide to use the old version of DOS. Conversely, deleting the contents of OLD_DOS.1 can save you about 1.75MB of useful disc space.

2. DIRECTORIES AND FILES

If you are using a system with normal capacity disc drives, then organising the files you keep on discs is relatively straight-forward. The usual method would be to keep similar applications on the same disc, so that one disc might contain files on word processing, another on spread sheets, and another on databases. MS-DOS keeps track of all such files by allocating space on each disc, called a directory, in which such information as the name of each file, its size, the date it was last amended, etc., is kept.

However, as you move up to systems with high-capacity disc drives (1.2 or 1.44 Mbyte floppies) and especially to systems with hard discs of 20, 50, 100 or more Mbytes, the amount of information you can store on them increases so much, that unless you organise the way you keep your files on such discs, you could easily spend all of your available time trying to find one.

The Directory Tree
MS-DOS can help you to organise your files on disc by providing a system of directories and subdirectories. The key to the DOS system is the 'root' directory, indicated by the back-slash sign (\), which is the main directory under which a number of subdirectories can be created. In turn, each subdirectory can have its own subdirectories, as shown here:

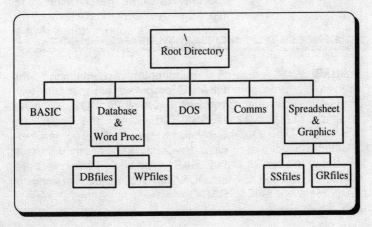

The root directory is shown with five subdirectories under it, while two of these have their own subdirectories below them. For maximum efficiency, the root directory should contain only the System and start up files, together with information on its subdirectories, a kind of an index drawer to a filing system.

Files in different subdirectories can have the same name because MS-DOS can be told which is which via a system of PATH names. For example, a file in the SSFILES sub-directory could have the same name, say SALARY.TMP, as one in the GRFILES subdirectory. Nevertheless, we can instruct MS-DOS to fetch the file in the SSFILES subdirectory by giving its path name which is:

```
\SPREADSH\SSFILES\SALARY.TMP
```

whereas that of the file in the GRFILES subdirectory is:

```
\SPREADSH\GRFILES\SALARY.TMP
```

In the example shown previously, the contents of the various subdirectories might be as follows:

\   The root directory, containing the two hidden System files MSDOS.SYS and IO.SYS, the Command Processor COMMAND.COM, the CONFIG.SYS file, the AUTOEXEC.BAT file, the names of all its subdirectories (five in our example).

BASIC   A subdirectory containing the QBASIC programs which came with version 5 and 6 of DOS, such as QBASIC.EXE and the help file QBASIC.HLP and any programs you write in QuickBasic which will have the .BAS extension. Earlier versions of DOS have different versions of BASIC.

DATABASE	A subdirectory containing a database with built-in word processor. Below this, there are two subdirectories; one for the database files (DBfiles), and one for the word processor files (WPfiles). The actual files in these subdirectories could have extensions which depend on the software.
DOS	A subdirectory containing all the MS-DOS files comprising the external MS-DOS commands.
COMMS	A subdirectory containing communications programs, proprietary backup software, etc.
SPREADSH	A subdirectory containing an integrated spreadsheet and graphics package. Below this, there are two subdirectories, one for the spread sheet files (SSfiles), and one for the graphics files (GRfiles). Again, the actual files in these could have different extensions which might be a function of the software package.

The Directory Listing

You could create the above directories with their subdirectories on your hard disc, but you might follow our example and set-up these on a floppy disc to avoid changing the configuration of your hard disc. Had you done so, typing the command DIR, displays what is shown on the next page.

The volume name (given on the display as MS-DOS_6) might be different in your case, as it depends on the label you gave your disc just after formatting. If you did not give a disc a label, then that line will read 'Volume in drive A has no label', assuming, of course, that you are accessing the A: drive.

```
C:\>dir a:

 Volume in drive A is MS-DOS_6
 Directory of A:\

COMMAND   COM       54,619 30/09/93    6:20
AUTOEXEC  BAT          640 09/11/93   19:42
CONFIG    SYS          361 09/11/93   19:42
BASIC        <DIR>         11/11/93   22:11
DATABASE     <DIR>         11/11/93   22:13
DOS          <DIR>         11/11/93   22:15
COMMS        <DIR>         11/11/93   22:16
SPREADSH     <DIR>         11/11/93   22:17
        8 file(s)       55,620 bytes
                       662,528 bytes free

C:\>
```

The second line of the display depends on your system and you have no control over it. Note that directories are distinguished from files in the directory listing by the inclusion of the letters <DIR> (in angled brackets) against their name. The order of their appearance depends on the order of their creation.

These days, many program packages create their own directory structure during installation and suggest names for the required directories and subdirectories into which they deposit their files. What they don't usually do, is to create subdirectories for your data. These you must create yourself in order to avoid adding your data files into the same directory as the one holding the program files. Doing so, makes it easier for you to make a back-up of your data files onto floppy discs, makes future upgrading of your programs easier and lays the foundation for a structured hard-disc system.

The TREE Command:

MS-DOS contains a very useful external command called 'tree'. Its use allows you to see pictorially the way DOS structures directories and subdirectories, as shown on the next page.

```
A:\>tree
Directory PATH listing for Volume MS-DOS_6
A:.
├──BASIC
├──DATABASE
│   ├──DBFILES
│   └──WPFILES
├──DOS
├──COMMS
└──SPREADSH
    ├──SSFILES
    └──GRFILES

A:\>
```

In versions of MS-DOS prior to version 4, this command produces only a character listing of directories and subdirectories, as opposed to the graphical visualisation which was introduced with the DOS version 4.0 and carried forward to later versions of the operating system.

The topmost level in a disc directory structure is the root directory which is created automatically by MS-DOS when you format a new disc and, unlike other directories, it does not have a unique name. It is within the root directory that you can create additional directories and subdirectories and give them unique names.

When you create directories and subdirectories, MS-DOS creates what is known as the dot (.) and double dot (..) entries. These shorthand notations can be used to identify the current and the parent directory, respectively. Thus, typing

DIR ..

at the DOS System prompt, lists the files in the parent directory of the current subdirectory on the logged disc drive.

Managing Directories

To manage directories you need to be able to create them, select them, and delete them. These three tasks can be carried out easily, as MS-DOS provides three special commands which can be used at the system prompt for the creation and management of directories. These are:

Command	Meaning	Example
MD	Make subdirectory	MD \BASIC
CD	Change directory	CD \BASIC
RD	Remove directory	RD \BASIC

The PROMPT Command:

However, before we explain these commands, make sure that your computer's prompt is of the form:

```
C:\>_
```

which indicates that the current directory is the root directory, shown by the back-slash (\). For the remainder of the book, we include the DOS prompt at the beginning of each command. DO NOT TYPE THESE PROMPTS, they should be already on the screen. Having a prompt which indicates in which directory we are at any given time is extremely useful and prudent because without it we could be copying files to the wrong subdirectory without realising it.

If your system is already configured, then an appropriate entry will exist within your AUTOEXEC.BAT file which produces this form of prompt. However, if this is not the case, then type

```
C:\>PROMPT $P$G
```

and press <Enter>.

The pg command should be in your AUTOEXEC.BAT file (to be discussed in a later chapter), but before you can do so, you will need to learn to use either the **Edit** screen editor (available to users of MS-DOS version 5 & 6, and to be discussed in Chapter 4) or any other editor or word processor, provided it can save files in text (ASCII) format.

Creating a Directory:

To create the subdirectory called BASIC from the system prompt, so that you can transfer to it all BASIC programs and files from the DOS subdirectory, type the following line

```
C:\>MD \BASIC
```

which makes the BASIC subdirectory in the root directory of the C: drive, and waits for further commands.

If you wanted to create this subdirectory on the A: drive, then you should have changed the logged drive first by typing

```
C:\>A:
A:\>_
```

and then issue the 'make directory' command.

In our example, the full path was given after the MD command, by first specifying the root directory with the use of the back-slash (\), followed by the name of the subdirectory.

To transfer files from the DOS subdirectory, first change directory using the CD command so that the logged directory is the target directory to which you will be copying the files, by typing

```
C:\>CD \BASIC
C:\BASIC>_
```

which causes the prompt to change, indicating that MS-DOS has actually changed directory. Without the prompt change, you would have had the typical 'where am I?' problem. Note that the moment we create a subdirectory we tend to refer to its parent as a directory, even though it might itself be a subdirectory of another parent directory.

To copy all BASIC programs and files from the \DOS directory to this new \BASIC directory, type

```
C:\BASIC>COPY C:\DOS\QBAS*.*
```

Alternatively, we could have issued this command from the root directory without first changing directories. In this case, the previous command would have to be typed as

```
C:\>COPY C:\DOS\QBAS*.* C:\BASIC
```

The first form of the COPY command says 'copy all files whose names start with QBAS from the \DOS directory to the logged directory', while the second form of the command says 'copy all files whose names start with QBAS from the \DOS directory to the \BASIC directory'.

Renaming Directories
Should you be dissatisfied with the name of an existing directory and you want to rename it, you can do so easily enough if you are a DOS 6 user. Pre-DOS 6 users must follow the slightly more complicated procedure, listed below.

DOS 6 Users

Use the **move** command. To find out everything there is to know about this command, type

C:\>**move /?**

or

C:|>**help move**

which causes the following help screen to be displayed:

```
C:\>move /?
Moves files and renames files and directories.

To move one or more files:
MOVE [/Y] [drive:][path]filename1[,...] destination

   /Y               Suppresses prompting to confirm creation of a directory.

To rename a directory:
MOVE [drive:][path]dirname1 dirname2

   [drive:][path]filename1  Specifies the location and name of the file
                            or files you want to move.
   destination              Specifies the new location of the file. Destination
                            can consist of a drive letter and colon, a directory
                            name, or a combination. If you are moving only one
                            file, you can also include a filename if you want
                            to rename the file when you move it.
   [drive:][path]dirname1   Specifies the directory you want to rename.
   dirname2                 Specifies the new name of the directory.

Note: If the destination you specify is an existing file, MOVE replaces
      that file with the file you are moving.

C:\>
```

A more detailed description of the Help System will be discussed shortly.

- Create another directory, giving it your preferred name,
- Copy to the newly created directory all the files from the unwanted directory,
- Delete all files from the unwanted directory,
- Remove the unwanted directory from its parent directory.

This procedure is essential because:

(a) Prior to MS-DOS 6 you could not rename directories from the system prompt,

(b) you could not remove directories unless they were empty.

As an example of the above procedure (whether you are a DOS 6 user or not, let us assume that we have created, as discussed previously, a subdirectory to the root directory, called DATA. To have created such a subdirectory, we would have had to return to the root directory from whichever subdirectory we were in at the time, by typing

```
CD \
```

at the DOS System prompt.

We now proceed to create a subdirectory to the DATA directory, called DOCS, by first changing directory from the root directory to that of DATA, as follows:

```
C:\>CD \DATA
C:\DATA>_
```

then make a subdirectory called DOCS by typing

```
C:\DATA>MD DOCS
```

at the prompt.

Note that we have not placed a back-slash in front of the new subdirectory name which causes it to be made in the currently logged directory. Had we included the back-slash, the subdirectory DOCS would have been created as a subdirectory of the root directory.

25

Alternatively, we could make DOCS without first changing directory by issuing the MD command from the root directory, but giving the full path specification. Having made the subdirectory DOCS, copy into it your files, as discussed previously.

Let us now assume that for some reason the directory name DOCS offends you and you would like to change it to WPDOCS instead. To do this you will have to type in the following commands, assuming you are at the root directory of the C: drive:

DOS 6 users

Type the following command:

```
C:\>move C:\DATA\DOCS C:\DATA\WPDOCS
```

the message c:\data\docs => c:\data\wpdocs [ok] confirms successful renaming.

Pre-DOS 6 users

Type the following commands:

```
C:\>CD \DATA
C:\DATA>MD WPDOCS
C:\DATA>COPY DOCS\*.* WPDOCS
C:\DATA>DEL DOCS\*.*
Are you sure? (Y/N)Y
C:\DATA>RD DOCS
C:\DATA>_
```

In order of appearance, these commands do the following:

    (a)   changes directory to DATA
    (b)   makes a subdirectory called WPDOCS
    (c)   copies from subdirectory DOCS all files to sub-directory WPDOCS
    (d)   deletes all files from the DOCS subdirectory
    (e)   MS-DOS asks for confirmation
    (f)   removes subdirectory DOCS.

Thus, restructuring directories, moving files from one directory to another, or making back-ups of groups of files, is much easier with DOS 6, or with the use of the DOS Shell (to be discussed next). However, the DOS Shell is only available to users of DOS version 4 or higher.

The Help System

Microsoft has greatly improved in MS-DOS 6 the HELP facility first introduced with DOS 5. It is now structured into Syntax, Notes and Examples. Typing **help** at the DOS prompt, displays the following screen:

```
 File  Search                                                    Help
                      MS-DOS Help: Command Reference
 Use the scroll bars to see more commands. Or, press the PAGE DOWN key. For
 more information about using MS-DOS Help, choose How to Use MS-DOS Help
 from the Help menu, or press F1. To exit MS-DOS Help, press ALT, F, X.

 <ANSI.SYS>              <Erase>                 <Multi-config>
 <Append>                <Exit>                  <Nlsfunc>
 <Attrib>                <Expand>                <Numlock>
 <Batch commands>        <Fasthelp>              <Path>
 <Break>                 <Fastopen>              <Pause>
 <Buffers>               <Fc>                    <Power>
 <Call>                  <Fcbs>                  <POWER.EXE>
 <Cd>                    <Fdisk>                 <Print>
 <Chcp>                  <Files>                 <Prompt>
 <Chdir>                 <Find>                  <Qbasic>
 <Chkdsk>                <For>                   <RAMDRIVE.SYS>
 <CHKSTATE.SYS>          <Format>                <Rd>
 <Choice>                <Goto>                  <Rem>
 <Cls>                   <Graphics>              <Ren>
 <Command>               <Help>                  <Rename>
 <CONFIG.SYS commands>   <HIMEM.SYS>             <Replace>
 <Copy>                  <If>                    <Restore>
 <Alt+C=Contents> <Alt+N=Next> <Alt+B=Back>            N 00006:002
```

The cursor (which is under the first item on the list) can be moved forward along the list by pressing the <Tab> key or backward by pressing <Shift+Tab>. You can even jump to a required item by specifying it in the displayed dialogue box when you choose **Search** from the menu bar. To print the displayed information on an item, use the **File, Print** option.

The HELP system supports hypertext links which let you jump from the current help screen to other related help screens. As an example, position the cursor under **ansi.sys** and press <Enter>. Immediately the help system will display the first of several help screens which relate to the selected item from the list, as shown on the next page.

27

```
 File  Search                                                              Help
                           MS-DOS Help: ANSI.SYS
 ◄Notes►  ◄Example►                                                           ░

                                ANSI.SYS

 Defines functions that change display graphics, control cursor movement, and
 reassign keys. The ANSI.SYS device driver supports ANSI terminal emulation
 of escape sequences to control your system's screen and keyboard. An ANSI
 escape sequence is a sequence of ASCII characters, the first two of which
 are the escape character (1Bh) and the left-bracket character (5Bh). The
 character or characters following the escape and left-bracket characters
 specify an alphanumeric code that controls a keyboard or display function.
 ANSI escape sequences distinguish between uppercase and lowercase letters;
 for example,"A" and "a" have completely different meanings.

 This device driver must be loaded by a <DEVICE> or <DEVICEHIGH> command in
 your CONFIG.SYS file.

 Note:  In this topic bold letters in syntax and ANSI escape sequences
        indicate text you must type exactly as it appears.

 Syntax
 <Alt+C=Contents> <Alt+N=Next> <Alt+B=Back>                      N 00001:002
```

To see the rest of the help screens, position the mouse
pointer (displayed as a small rectangle) on the scroll bar
under the position indicator and press the left mouse button.

Note the words <DEVICE> and <DEVICEHIGH> towards
the bottom of the first help screen above. The angle brackets
indicate hypertext links. Position the mouse pointer on
<DEVICE> and press the left mouse button. Immediately the
HELP system jumps to the new item, as shown below:

```
 File  Search                                                              Help
                           MS-DOS Help: DEVICE
 ◄Notes►  ◄Example►                                                           ░

                                DEVICE

 Loads the device driver you specify into memory. You can use this command
 only in your CONFIG.SYS file.

 Syntax

     DEVICE=[drive:][path]filename [dd-parameters]

 Parameters

 [drive:][path]filename
     Specifies the location and name of the device driver you want to load.

 [dd-parameters]
     Specifies any command-line information required by the device driver.

 Related Command

 <Alt+C=Contents> <Alt+N=Next> <Alt+B=Back>                      N 00001:002
```

28

To save having to go through the index, you can obtain help screens directly by typing **help** followed a specific command. For example, typing

    help copy

will produce the help screens relating to the copy command.

To obtain a shorter listing of all DOS commands, use the **fasthelp** command. Thus, typing

    fasthelp

at the DOS command prompt, displays the following information:

```
For more information on a specific command, type FASTHELP command-name.
APPEND    Allows programs to open data files in specified directories as if
          they were in the current directory.
ATTRIB    Displays or changes file attributes.
BREAK     Sets or clears extended CTRL+C checking.
CD        Displays the name of or changes the current directory.
CHCP      Displays or sets the active code page number.
CHDIR     Displays the name of or changes the current directory.
CHKDSK    Checks a disk and displays a status report.
CLS       Clears the screen.
COMMAND   Starts a new instance of the MS-DOS command interpreter.
COMP      Compares the contents of two files or sets of files.
COPY      Copies one or more files to another location.
CTTY      Changes the terminal device used to control your system.
DATE      Displays or sets the date.
DBLSPACE  Sets up or configures DoubleSpace compressed drives.
DEBUG     Starts Debug, a program testing and editing tool.
DEFRAG    Reorganizes the files on a disk to optimize the disk.
DEL       Deletes one or more files.
DELOLDOS  Deletes the OLD_DOS.1 directory and the files it contains.
DELTREE   Deletes a directory and all the files and subdirectories in it.
DIR       Displays a list of files and subdirectories in a directory.
DISKCOMP  Compares the contents of two floppy disks.
---More---
```

Finally, you can obtained a quick listing of all command switches, etc., with the prompt available so that you can build up your own command on screen without having to make notes on paper, by typing the command, followed by the string </?>. For example, typing

    copy /?

at the DOS command prompt, produces the following information:

```
C:\>copy /?
Copies one or more files to another location.

COPY [/A | /B] source [/A | /B] [+ source [/A | /B] [+ ...]] [destination
[/A | /B]] [/V]

  source       Specifies the file or files to be copied.
  /A           Indicates an ASCII text file.
  /B           Indicates a binary file.
  destination  Specifies the directory and/or filename for the new file(s).
  /V           Verifies that new files are written correctly.

To append files, specify a single file for destination, but multiple files
for source (using wildcards or file1+file2+file3 format).

C:\>
```

You can even obtain help on Help. To do this, type

help

at the DOS command prompt, then select **Help** from the menu options at the top-right corner of the Help screen, to display the following information:

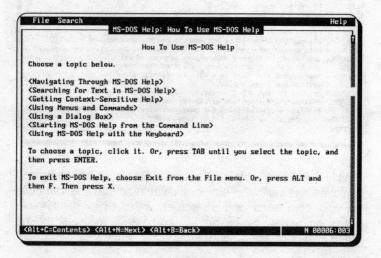

```
 File  Search                                                       Help
                        MS-DOS Help: How To Use MS-DOS Help

                           How To Use MS-DOS Help

   Choose a topic below.

   <Navigating Through MS-DOS Help>
   <Searching for Text in MS-DOS Help>
   <Getting Context-Sensitive Help>
   <Using Menus and Commands>
   <Using a Dialog Box>
   <Starting MS-DOS Help from the Command Line>
   <Using MS-DOS Help with the Keyboard>

   To choose a topic, click it. Or, press TAB until you select the topic, and
   then press ENTER.

   To exit MS-DOS Help, choose Exit from the File menu. Or, press ALT and
   then F. Then press X.

 <Alt+C=Contents> <Alt+N=Next> <Alt+B=Back>                   N 00006:003
```

As you can see, the Help System of MS-DOS 6 is extremely usable. Unfortunately the additional MS-DOS 6 Utilities, such as MSBACKUP, have their own help facilities which are not integrated with the main MS-DOS Help System.

Using the DOS Shell

The DOS Shell is not distributed with MS-DOS 6.2, but is with versions 4.0 to 6.0. If you have the program and type DOSSHELL at the C> prompt, then you will be able to see the directory tree which is displayed on the top-left part of the DOS Shell screen with a listing of the files of the logged directory (in this case the root directory) appearing on the top-right of the screen, as shown below.

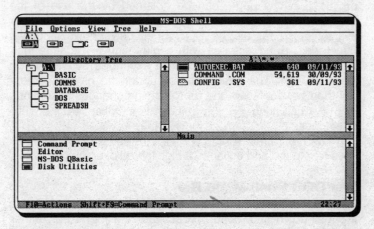

You can navigate around the DOS Shell screen, either by using the keyboard or by using a mouse.

To select an item with the keyboard, use the <Tab> key to move the cursor between screen areas, then use the vertical arrow keys to highlight the required item within the selected area and press <Enter>.

To select an item with the mouse, simply point to the required item and click the left mouse button. It is assumed, of course, that the required mouse driver is loaded according to the instructions that accompany the device. This requires you to include the command **MOUSE** within your AUTOEXEC.BAT file (more about this later).

If you have an EGA or VGA screen, the mouse pointer appears as an inclined arrow, indicating that DOS Shell is in 'Graphics' mode, otherwise for a CGA screen it appears as a small square, indicating that DOS Shell is in 'Text' mode. You can change modes by using the <Alt+O> command (press the <Alt> key and while holding it down, press the letter <O>) to reveal the pull-down **Options** menu and select the **Display** option, either by pointing with the mouse and clicking the left mouse button, or by using the down arrow key to highlight it and pressing <Enter>. A selection box appears in the middle of the screen from which you can select the required mode.

As seen earlier, the same directory tree as the one shown on the previous page, can be obtained by the use of the external DOS command 'tree'. The two directory trees differ slightly in so far as the DOS Shell only shows first-level directories. Subdirectories with a plus sign (+) against their name in the directory tree, can be expanded by clicking on the plus sign. The subdirectories under the given directory will then be displayed and the plus sign changes to a minus sign (−). Clicking on the minus sign collapses the sub-directories.

If you don't have a mouse, use the grey <+> or grey <−> keys to expand and collapse a highlighted directory.

The DOS Shell Menu Bar

Each menu bar option on the DOS Shell has associated with it a pull-down sub-menu. To activate the menu bar, either press the <Alt> key, which causes the first item on the menu bar (in this case **File**) to be highlighted, then use the right and left arrow keys to highlight any of the items of the menu bar, or use the mouse to point to an item. Pressing either <Enter> or the left mouse button, reveals the pull-down sub-menu.

The pull-down sub-menus can also be activated directly by pressing the <Alt> key followed by the first letter of the required menu option. Thus pressing <Alt+O>, causes the **Options** sub-menu to be displayed. Use the up and down arrow keys to move the highlighted bar up and down within a sub-menu, or the right and left arrow keys to move along the options of the menu bar. Pressing the <Enter> key selects the highlighted option, while pressing the <Esc> key closes the menu system.

The Menu Bar Options:

Each item of the menu bar offers several options which are described on the following pages. However, dimmed or not visible command names indicate that these commands are unavailable at this time; you might need to select an item before you can use such commands. The biggest difference is observed with the **Files** sub-menu and it depends on whether you are working with files or programs (you have more options available to you with files).

You can display the information given below by selecting the DOS Shell **Help, Commands** option which causes a File List and a Program List to appear on your screen. Choosing an item from these lists (by highlighting it and pressing <Enter>, or pointing at it and clicking the left mouse button) produces the information on the specific item. This same information is listed below which should make reference to it easier to access.

The File Menu with Files

When DOS Shell is first entered, or if you select an item from the File-list area, such as the AUTOEXEC.BAT file, and then choose **File**, the following menu is displayed:

Open: Starts a selected program and an associated file, if there is one.

Run: Displays a dialogue box in which you type the name of the program file that starts the program.

Print: Prints the selected text file(s). The Print command only works if you have run PRINT.COM at the command prompt.

```
┌─ File ──────────────────┐
│ Open                    │
│ Run...                  │
│ Print                   │
│ Associate...            │
│ Search...               │
│ View File Contents   F9 │
├─────────────────────────┤
│ Move...              F7 │
│ Copy...              F8 │
│ Delete...            Del│
│ Rename...               │
│ Change Attributes...    │
├─────────────────────────┤
│ Create Directory...     │
├─────────────────────────┤
│ Select All              │
│ Deselect All            │
├─────────────────────────┤
│ Exit             Alt+F4 │
└─────────────────────────┘
```

Associate: Associates all files having the same extension with a program, or a selected file with a program so that starting the program automatically loads the specified file.

Search: Finds files on all or part of the currently selected disc drive.

33

View File Contents: Displays the contents of the selected text file or binary file.

Move: Moves the selected file(s) from one directory to a directory you specify.

Copy: Copies one or more files in one directory to a directory you specify.

Delete: Deletes selected files or directories.

Rename: Renames a selected file or directory to the name you specify.

Change Attributes: Displays the attributes assigned to a file, such as Hidden, System, Archive, and Read-Only. Use this command to change these attributes.

Create Directory: Creates a new directory on the current drive. If a directory is selected, it creates a subdirectory within that directory.

Select All: Selects all files in the currently selected directory.

Deselect All: Cancels all selections except one in the currently selected directory.

Exit: Quits DOS Shell and returns to the system prompt.

The File Menu with Programs

If you select an item from the Program-list area of the Main group of programs, such as the **Editor**, and then choose **File,** the following menu is displayed:

New: Adds a new group or program item to the currently selected group.

Open: Starts a program and an associated file (if any), or displays the contents of a group.

Copy: Copies a program item to the group you specify.

```
┌─────────────────────────┐
│ █ File                  │
├─────────────────────────┤
│ New...                  │
│ Open           Enter    │
│ Copy                    │
│ Delete...      Del      │
│ Properties...           │
│ Reorder                 │
├─────────────────────────┤
│ Run...                  │
├─────────────────────────┤
│ Exit          Alt+F4    │
└─────────────────────────┘
```

After choosing the command, open the group you want to copy to, and then press **F2**.

Delete: Deletes the selected group, or program item, from a group. Before deleting a group, you must delete all of its program items.

Properties: Specifies for a program item, the title, the command that starts the program, the start-up directory for the program to use, an application shortcut key, Help text, a password, and other properties.

Reorder: Moves the selected program item or group from its current location to the location you specify.

Run: Displays a dialogue box in which you type the name of the program file that starts the program.

Exit: Quits DOS Shell and returns to the system prompt.

Options Menu:
Selecting **Options** when working with either files or programs, displays the following pull-down menu:

Confirmation: Specifies if DOS Shell should prompt you for confirmation before deleting files or replacing files with duplicate names.

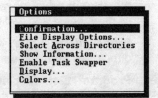

File Display Options: Lists files in sequence by name, extension, date, size, or order on disc. Also controls the display of Hidden or System files.

Select Across Directories: Controls whether or not you can select files in more than one directory. A mark next to the command indicates that it is active.

Show Information: Displays information on the selected file(s), directory and disc.

Enable Task Swapper: Turns on or off task swapping and displays the Active Task List to the right of the Program List. With this on, you can have more than one program open at a time and switch between them. A mark next to the command indicates that it is on.

Display: Changes screen mode and the resolution used to display DOS Shell.

Colors: Changes the colour scheme used for DOS Shell.

View Menu:

Selecting **View** when working with either files or programs, displays a pull-down menu. With files, there is an additional 'Refresh' command, as shown below:

Single File List: Displays a single directory tree and file list for the current drive.

```
View
┌──────────────────────────┐
│ Single File List         │
│ Dual File Lists          │
│ All Files                │
│ Program/File Lists       │
│ Program List             │
│                          │
│ Repaint Screen  Shift+F5 │
│ Refresh         F5       │
└──────────────────────────┘
```

Dual File List: Displays two directory trees and file lists for the selected drive(s) in the file list.

All Files: Lists every file on the current drive, as well as information about the drive, its directories, and its files.

Program/File Lists: Causes the display of a list of directories and files and a list of groups and programs.

Program List: Displays a list of groups and program items in the current group.

Repaint Screen: Redraws the screen, but does not update the list of files. For the latter to happen, use the 'Refresh' command.

Refresh: Rereads the disc and updates the list to show changes caused by such actions as deleting or restoring files.

Tree Menu

This menu option is only available when you are working with files. Selecting **Tree** displays the following pull-down menu.

Expand One Level: Displays the next level of sub-directories for the selected directory in the Directory tree.

Expand Branch: Displays all levels of subdirectories in the selected directory in the Directory Tree.

Expand All: Displays all subdirectories in the Directory Tree.

Collapse Branch: Hides all currently displayed sub-directories in the selected directory in the Directory Tree.

Help Menu

Selecting **Help** when working with either files or programs, displays the following pull-down menu:

Index: Displays the DOS Shell Help Index.

Keyboard: Displays a list of shortcut keys you can use with DOS Shell.

Shell Basics: Displays a list of topics for basic skills you need to work with DOS Shell.

Commands: Displays a list of all DOS Shell commands, grouped by menu.

Procedures: Displays a list of topics you can look at for help on DOS Shell tasks.

Using Help: Displays a list of topics which explain how to use DOS Shell Help.

File Selection in DOS Shell:

To select a single file or multiple files while in DOS Shell, use either the mouse or the keyboard. The procedure is as follows:

- To select a single file: With the mouse, click the name of the file, while with the keyboard use the arrow keys to highlight it.

- To select two or more contiguous files: With the mouse, click the first filename you want to select, then press down the <Shift> key while you click the last filename of the block. With the keyboard, use the arrow keys to highlight the first filename in the list, then press down the <Shift> key and while holding it down use the arrow keys to highlight the block of filenames.

- To select two or more non-contiguous files: With the mouse, press and hold down the <Ctrl> key while you click at the required filenames, while with the keyboard select the first filename then press <Shift+**F8**> and move to the next filename, press the <Spacebar> to select the highlighted filename, go the next filename and press <Spacebar>, and so on, until you have finished when you press <Shift+**F8**>.

The DOS Shell, gives a graphical way of easily manipulating your files and directories, without having to learn all the command names. There is a down side though; while it is active it uses valuable RAM memory. You may not be able to use it and run very large application programs at the same time.

3. MANAGING DISC FILES

MS-DOS provides several commands which help you to manage your disc files efficiently. Some of these commands are internal and some are external. If the commands under discussion are external commands and your computer is a twin floppy system, it will be pointed out to you so you can insert the System disc (the floppy disc on which you have installed MS-DOS - refer to the FORMAT and the SYS commands) in the logged drive, which is the drive indicated by letter on the screen prompt.

The FORMAT Command

One of the first things you will need to do, as a new user, is to make a working copy of your system disc, or favoured software package, or just a back-up copy of your programs or data. Such packages and/or data are far too valuable in terms of money, or time invested in producing them to be used continually without the safeguard of back-up copies.

Again, it is assumed that in the case of a hard disc-based system, your hard disc has already been formatted according to your manufacturer's instructions when setting up the system, and that all the MS-DOS external command files have been transferred onto it.

A new floppy disc must be formatted before it can be used by your computer's operating system. A floppy disc that has been formatted in one computer, can only be used in another computer if they are compatible and use the same operating system.

To format a disc, in the case of a hard disc system where the logged drive will be drive C:, insert the new floppy disc in the A: drive and type

```
C:\>FORMAT A:/S/V
```

In the case of a twin floppy system, insert the system start-up disc in the A: drive, as FORMAT is an external command and needs to be loaded into RAM from the system disc, then insert the new floppy disc in the B: drive and type

```
A:\>FORMAT B:/S/V
```

Drive C: (or A: in the case of a floppy disc) is accessed momentarily, the FORMAT utility file is loaded into RAM and executed. You are then given instructions to insert a floppy disc in drive A: (or B: in the case of a twin floppy disc system), and press <Enter> to begin. Be very careful never to format the wrong disc (particularly the C: drive), as *all* files that might be on it will be lost.

The two switches, typed after the slash character (/), have the following meaning:

The /s switch instructs MS-DOS to copy the hidden system files and the COMMAND.COM file onto the newly formatted disc. This will be required if you intend to use the disc to boot up the system, but otherwise is not required.

The /v switch allows you to give a volume label to your new disc, after formatting is completed.

These and other available switches will be discussed shortly. If you are using MS-DOS 5 or 6, typing

FORMAT /?

displays the following help screen:

```
C:\>format /?
Formats a disk for use with MS-DOS.

FORMAT drive: [/V[:label]] [/Q] [/U] [/F:size] [/B | /S]
FORMAT drive: [/V[:label]] [/Q] [/U] [/T:tracks /N:sectors] [/B | /S]
FORMAT drive: [/V[:label]] [/Q] [/U] [/1] [/4] [/B | /S]
FORMAT drive: [/Q] [/U] [/1] [/4] [/8] [/B | /S]

  /V[:label]  Specifies the volume label.
  /Q          Performs a quick format.
  /U          Performs an unconditional format.
  /F:size     Specifies the size of the floppy disk to format (such
              as 160, 180, 320, 360, 720, 1.2, 1.44, 2.88).
  /B          Allocates space on the formatted disk for system files.
  /S          Copies system files to the formatted disk.
  /T:tracks   Specifies the number of tracks per disk side.
  /N:sectors  Specifies the number of sectors per track.
  /1          Formats a single side of a floppy disk.
  /4          Formats a 5.25-inch 360K floppy disk in a high-density drive.
  /8          Formats eight sectors per track.

C:\>
```

Such help screens are available for all MS-DOS 5 and 6 commands, but not for earlier versions of the operating system. For this very reason, we tend to give as thorough an explanation of these commands, as thought necessary.

Instructions on commands for users of the DOS Shell are given as shown below:

DOS Shell =>   To format a floppy disc when using
                DOS Shell, use the **Disk Utilities,
                Format** command, as follows:

Select the **Disk Utilities** option from the Main group of programs, shown below:

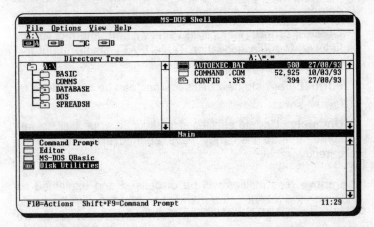

The selection can be achieved by double-clicking at the required option which causes the pull-down menu, shown below, to appear on the screen:

If you have installed DOS 6 without upgrading from an earlier version of DOS, then the two entries 'Backup Fixed Disk' and 'Restore Fixed Disk' will not be displayed in DOS Shell's Disk Utilities.

From this latter screen, double-click at the **Format** command, and follow the instruction given on the screen.

41

The other options on the 'Disk Utilities' menu perform the following tasks:

Main: Returns you to the Main group of programs.

Disk Copy: Copies the contents of a floppy disc to another floppy disc.

Backup Fixed Disk & Restore Fixed Disk: Copies and restores files for pre-DOS 6 users from/to the hard disc onto/from several consecutively numbered floppy discs.

Quick Format: Reformats already formatted discs by deleting the File Allocation Table (FAT) - more about this later.

Format: Formats new discs so they can be recognised by MS-DOS.

Undelete: Undeletes files. However, if your disc is full, some deleted files may have been overwritten and be unrecoverable.

The above disc utilities will be discussed and explained as and when the relevant commands are introduced in the book. They were listed above all together for convenience, as we were discussing the disc utilities available with DOS Shell.

Type and Size of Discs:

There are some additional switches that can be used with the FORMAT command (whether you are using DOS Shell or not) which, however, are dependent on the type of disc drive being used and size of disc. These are as follows:

Disc type	Disc size	Switches
160/180 KB	5 ¼ "	/f:size, /b, /s, /u, /q, /1, /8, /4
320/360 KB	5 ¼ "	/f:size, /b, /s, /u, /q, /1, /8, /4
1.2 MB	5 ¼ "	/f:size, /b, /s, /u, /q, /4, /t, /n
720 KB/1.44 MB	3 ½ "	/f:size, /b, /s, /u, /q, /t, /n
2.88 MB	3 ½ "	/f:size, /b, /s, /u, /q.

where

/f:*size* specifies the size of the floppy disc to format. This switch can be used instead of the /t and /n switches. Use one of the following values for size, which specifies the capacity of the disc in Kbytes:

160/180; single-sided, double-density 5¼" discs,
320/360; double-sided, double-density 5¼" discs,
720; double-sided, double-density 3½" discs,
1200; double-sided, high-density 5¼" discs,
1440; double-sided, high-density 3½" discs,
2880; 2.88 MB, double-sided, 3½" discs.

/b   reserves space for the system files IO.SYS and MSDOS.SYS on a newly formatted disc

/s   copies the operating system files IO.SYS, MSDOS.SYS, and COMMAND.COM from the system's start-up drive to the newly formatted disc

/u   specifies an unconditional format operation for a disc, which destroys all existing data on the disc and prevents you from later unformatting the disc

/q   deletes the file allocation table (FAT) and the root directory of a previously formatted disc, but does not scan the disc for bad sectors

/1   formats only one side of the disc (seldom used)

/8   formats 8 sectors per track (seldom used)

/4   formats 40 tracks with 9 sectors per track for 360 Kbytes using a 1.2 Mbyte high-capacity disc drive. This switch must be used if you are using double-density, but not high-capacity discs in a 1.2 Mbyte drive

/t   specifies the number of tracks, written as /t:40 for forty tracks. To format a 720 Kbytes double-sided disc in a high-capacity 3.5" disc drive (1.44 Mbytes), use switches t:80/n:9

/n   specifies the number of sectors per track to format, written as /n:9 for nine sectors.

Switches f:*size*, /b, /u, and /q, are new to MS-DOS 5, while switches /1, /4, and /8 are kept for backward compatibility to earlier versions of DOS. If switches /t or /n are specified, then both parameters must be entered. All other switches can be used separately or omitted altogether from the command. Omitting the /s switch from this command saves disc space.

The SYS Command

Should you change your mind after you have formatted a disc without the use of the /s switch, you can use the external SYS command to transfer the system files from the system start-up drive onto a previously formatted disc, inserted in another drive. The command takes the form:

C:\>**SYS A:** in the case of a hard disc based system, or

A:\>**SYS B:** in the case of a floppy disc based system.

To successfully transfer the operating system to a disc with this method, the disc must either be newly formatted or else have space on it for the transfer of the operating system, by perhaps already having a different version of it on the target disc, or by having used the /u switch.

The order in which files are copied is: IO.SYS, MSDOS.SYS, and COMMAND.COM. If your system is using DBLSPACE, the file DBLSPACE.BIN will also be copied to give a bootable floppy disc that supports your compressed discs.

Differences Between Disc Drives:

The PC, XT and compatibles have 360 Kbyte double-sided, double-density disc drives. Discs are formatted with 40 tracks per side, 9 sectors per track with 0.5 Kbyte of information per sector, resulting in 360 Kbyte capacity.

The IBM AT, XT286 and compatibles have 1.2 Mbytes double-sided, high-capacity disc drives. Discs are formatted with 80 tracks per side, 15 sectors per track with 0.5 Kbyte of information per sector resulting in 1.2 Mbytes capacity. However, each track takes the same physical space as that of the 360 Kbyte drive, the difference being that the tracks are half the width of the 360 Kbyte drive.

44

Discs formatted on 1.2 Mbyte disc drives with the /4 switch use only one half of the width of each of the 40 tracks. This information can easily be read by a 360 Kbyte drive (as a result of tolerance in signal level), provided the other half of the track is completely clear. Should you now use the 360 Kbyte drive to write to the disc, information is written to the full width of the track which can still be read by the 1.2 Mbyte disc drive (again, as a result of tolerance in signal level).

However, any subsequent writing to such a disc using the 1.2 Mbyte drive, results in changes to only one half of the track width. The result is half a track containing the new information with the corresponding other half of the same track containing the old, half-overwritten information, which makes it impossible for the 360 Kbyte disc drive to make any sense of it. Thus, to avoid such incompatibility between disc drives, always format double-density discs in a 360 Kbyte drive. Attempting to format a double-density disc to 1.2 Mbytes will result in many bad sectors with future loss of data becoming highly possible.

There are no such problems arising from the use of 3.5" discs which have been formatted as 720 Kbytes in a high-capacity (1.44 Mbytes) disc drive and subsequently used to read or write to them by either a 720 Kbyte or a 1.44 Mbyte disc drive. Again, avoid formatting non high-density discs to 1.44 Mbytes. If you do so accidentally, (this can happen if you use the DISKCOPY command with earlier versions of DOS to copy files from a 720 Kbytes disc to a high-capacity disc), do not attempt to reformat the high-capacity disc to 1.44 Mbytes, because the higher current used by the disc drive to format it to 720 Kbytes can not be wiped out by the reformatting process.

The COPY Command

To copy all files on the disc in the logged drive to the disc in the A: drive, type

```
C:\>COPY *.* A:
```

Note the most useful three-character combination in MS-DOS, namely *.* which means 'all filenames with all extensions'.

However, if you wanted to copy a set of files from drive A: to drive C:, while being logged onto the C: drive, type

```
C:\>COPY A:*.DOC C:
```

which means 'copy from the A: drive all the files with extension .DOC to the C: drive'.

The /v switch can be used at the end of the COPY command to force MS-DOS to verify that the file(s) it has copied can be read. For example,

```
C:\>COPY \DOS\FORMAT.COM A:/V
```

will copy the formatting utility file FORMAT.COM from the \DOS directory of the logged drive to the A: drive and force verification that the file can be read.

```
┌─────────────────────────────────────────────────────┐
│              ▄▄▄▄▄▄ File Display Options ▄▄▄▄▄▄       │
│   ┌───────────────────────────────────────────────┐  │
│   │ Name:   *.*_                                   │  │
│   │                                                │  │
│   │                              Sort by:          │  │
│   │ [ ] Display hidden/system files  ● Name        │  │
│   │                                  ○ Extension   │  │
│   │                                  ○ Date        │  │
│   │ [ ] Descending order             ○ Size        │  │
│   │                                  ○ DiskOrder    │  │
│   │                                                │  │
│   │   ( OK )      ( Cancel )      ( Help )          │  │
│   └───────────────────────────────────────────────┘  │
└─────────────────────────────────────────────────────┘
```

DOS Shell =>   To copy files when using DOS Shell, select the file(s) you want to copy, then use the **File, Copy** command.

To change the default selection of files when using DOS Shell, use the **Options, File Display Options** command. This displays the following dialogue box:

The DISKCOPY Command

Both the formatting and copying can be done in one go by using the DISKCOPY command, as follows:

```
C:\>DISKCOPY A: B:
```

which will copy all the files and subdirectories from the A: drive, to the B: drive and format the disk in the B: drive at the same time, if it is not already formatted.

However, if the disc in the B: drive is already formatted, but at different capacity to that in the A: drive, and you are using a version of DOS prior to version 5.0, then the disc in the B: drive is reformatted to the same capacity as that in the A: drive. This problem has been overcome with MS-DOS version 5 and 6.

You can not use the DISKCOPY command to copy files from a floppy disc to a hard disc, or to copy files between two floppy discs of different size (such as 3½" and 5¼" discs).

Note: Sometimes it is preferable to use the FORMAT and COPY commands than use the DISKCOPY command when copying all files from one disc to another. The reason is that bad sectors are frozen out when formatting a disc with the FORMAT command and the subsequent use of COPY, avoids these sectors. The DISKCOPY command on the other hand, seeks to make an identical copy (sector by sector) of the original disc which means that it attempts to write on bad sectors, if any, which might lead to an unsuccessful copy operation.

DOS Shell =>   To copy all files from one disc to another when using DOS Shell, use the **Disk Copy** program in the Disk Utilities.

The DISKCOMP Command

This external utility is mostly needed if you use the DISKCOPY command. The command compares the contents of two discs, and takes the following form:

`C:\>DISKCOMP A: B:`   compares the discs in the A: and the B: drives. For single floppy drive systems use A: A:, in which case you will be prompted to insert each disc, as required.

The DELETE & UNDELETE Commands

Unwanted files on a disc can be deleted, as follows:

`C:\>DEL EXAMPLE.TMP`   deletes EXAMPLE.TMP on the root directory of the C: drive

`C:\>DEL A:EXAMPLE.TMP`   deletes EXAMPLE.TMP on the A: drive

`A:\>DEL *.*`   deletes all files on the logged drive.

Luckily, the use of the DEL *.* command evokes the response

`Are you sure? (Y/N)`

which acts as a safety net. It is a good idea to always check what you are about to delete from your disc by first using the DIR command.

For example, say you intend to delete all the .TMP files from your disc. First use DIR *.TMP and if what is displayed on screen is what you want to delete, then type DEL and press the **F3** function key. This has the effect of displaying on the screen the last command you typed on the keyboard, minus the characters you typed prior to pressing the **F3** key. Thus, DEL replaces DIR and the use of **F3** displays the rest of the command. In this way you avoid making any mistakes by re-typing.

As you will, no doubt, use this command at some time or other on your C: drive, it would be prudent to copy both your AUTOEXEC.BAT and CONFIG.SYS files into your DOS directory. In this way you will have copies of these vital files away from harm's reach!

DOS Shell =>   To delete files when using DOS Shell, select the file(s) you want to delete, then use the **File, Delete** command.

With MS-DOS 5 and 6, you can use the UNDELETE command to recover deleted files. To test this command, first make a copy of your AUTOEXEC.BAT file by typing:

`C:\>COPY AUTOEXEC.BAT TEST`

or using the **File, Copy** command from within DOS Shell. Then, use the **Delete** command to delete the file TEST.

To undelete a deleted file, type the command

```
C:\>UNDELETE TEST
```

at the C:\> prompt. This causes DOS to display the following information:

```
UNDELETE - A delete protection facility
Copyright (C) 1987-1993 Central Point Software, Inc.
All rights reserved.

Directory: C:\
File Specifications: TEST.*

    Delete Sentry control file not found.

    Deletion-tracking file not found.

    MS-DOS directory contains    1 deleted files.
    Of those,    1 files may be recovered.

Using the MS-DOS directory method.

    ?EST              640  9/11/93 19:42   ...A  Undelete (Y/N)?y
    Please type the first character for ?EST    . : t

File successfully undeleted.
```

DOS Shell =>   To undelete a file when using DOS Shell, use the **Disk Utilities, Undelete** command.

The pop-up dialogue box offers you the switch **/LIST** which, however, only causes DOS to list the files that can be undeleted without actually recovering them. The following three additional switches can be used to recover files:

/all   recovers deleted files without prompting for confirmation on each file

/dos   recovers files that are internally listed as deleted by DOS, prompting for confirmation on each file

/dt   recovers only those files listed in the deletion-tracking file, prompting for confirmation on each file.

For additional information on **Undelete**, see Chapter 7.

The RENAME Command

The REN command is used to rename files. As an example, let us assume that we want to rename a file on the disc in the logged drive from its current filename OLDFILE.DOC to the new filename NEWFILE.DOC. This can be done as follows:

```
C:\>REN OLDFILE.DOC NEWFILE.DOC
```

Note the importance of spaces after REN and in between the two file names. The command can be interpreted as:

```
Rename from filename1 to filename2
```

To rename a file on a disc in a disc drive other than the logged drive, the disc drive specification must also be included in the command, as follows:

```
C:\>REN A:OLDFILE.DOC NEWFILE.DOC
```

Note that, if you intend to rename a file and give it a filename that already exists on disc, you must first delete the unwanted file before renaming, otherwise MS-DOS will refuse to obey your command, informing you that the filename you have chosen already exists on disc.

> DOS Shell => To rename a file when using DOS Shell, select the file you want to rename, then use the **File, Rename** command.

The CHKDSK & SCANDISK Commands

CHKDSK is the old disc-checking program found in all pre-DOS 6.2 versions. In MS-DOS 6.2 it has been replaced by SCANDISK which works on both compressed and uncompressed drives and, in fact, offers much more than CHKDSK.

Each disc has a file allocation table (FAT) where a note is kept of which clusters have been allocated to which file. However, with heavy disc use, the file allocation table can be corrupted and using CHKDSK will report 'lost clusters found'. The additional /f switch, allows CHKDSK to also do some routine maintenance, namely fixing lost clusters. A cluster is the minimum amount of space (one or more sectors) that can be allocated to a file on disc. The /f switch converts these into files and gives them the general name FILExxxx.CHK, where xxxx starts with 0000 and increments by 1. These files can then be checked and perhaps deleted if found to be useless.

The command takes the form:

```
C:\>CHKDSK /f
```

which checks the disc in the logged drive.

SCANDISK, like CHKDSK can detect cross links, but it can also repair the files corrupted by cross linking in the data structure of both compressed and uncompressed discs. The program checks the 'Media descriptor', the 'File allocation tables', the 'Directory structure', the 'File system', and performs a 'Surface scan'. To run the program, type SCANDISK at the command prompt.

The XCOPY Command

The XCOPY command allows us to copy files and directories, including lower level subdirectories, if they exist, to the specified destination drive and directory. The command takes the following form:

```
C:\>XCOPY source_filespec destination [switches]
```

where *source_filespec* specifies the source file or drive and directory you want to copy and *destination* can be the drive to which you want this source file to be copied to. For example,

```
C:\>XCOPY A:*.* B:
```

will copy all files in the A: drive to the B: drive. If you only have one floppy drive, you will be prompted to change discs.

Some of the *switches* available (for a full list see the 'Command Summary' section) are as follows:

/d   copies source files which were modified on or after a specified date

/p   prompts the user with '(Y/N?)' before copying files

/s   copies directories and their subdirectories unless they are empty

/v   causes verification of each file as it is written.

XCOPY copies all files and subdirectories in the specified directory (except hidden and system files) from one disc to another by reading from the source disc as many files as possible into memory, then copying them to the target disc. This is unlike the COPY command which copies each file in turn, therefore, taking much longer. However, when the target disc becomes full, XCOPY stops and does not ask for another disc to be inserted in the target drive. XCOPY can copy files even when the two discs are of different format, unlike the DISKCOPY command which requires that the source and target disc be the same format.

If you do not specify a path in the source filespec, XCOPY starts from the current directory. If you specify only a drive or path, but no files, XCOPY assumes you mean 'all files'. You can specify a target filename that is different from the source filename which causes files to be renamed while copying.

Backing-up & Restoring Hard Discs

MS-DOS 6 employs a new utility, called MSBACKUP, for backing-up and restoring hard discs. This utility will be discussed in Chapter 7. However, for the sake of completeness, the pre-DOS 6 BACKUP and RESTORE commands are discussed below. The external RESTORE command is included with DOS 6 to enable DOS 5 and earlier backups to be restored.

Since a hard disc contains valuable information, you must make additional copies of all your important files. The pre-DOS 6 BACKUP command and the DOS 6 MSBACKUP utility allow you to archive files and generate those back-up copies on floppy discs. If you have a hard disc, you should back-up your data often; daily or weekly, if necessary. The pre-DOS 6 BACKUP command takes the form:

BACKUP *source destination switches*

where *source* is the drive/path/files to be backed up,
destination is the drive to back-up to, and
switches are:

/a to add the files to a disc in the destination drive

/d:*date* to back-up only files modified at or after the specified date

/f:*size* to cause the target disc to be formatted to a size which is different from the default size of the disc drive. Use one of the following values for size, which specifies the capacity of the disc in Kbytes:

160/180; single-sided, double-density 5¼" discs,
320/360; double-sided, double-density 5¼" discs,
720; double-sided, double-density 3½" discs,
1200; double-sided, high-density 5¼" discs,
1440; double-sided, high-density 3½" discs,
2880; 2.88 MB, double-sided, 3½" discs.
/m to back-up only files modified since they were last backed up

/s to also back-up subdirectories of the source path

/t: *time* to back-up only files modified at or after the specified time

/L: *filename* to create a log file, called *filename*, in which is stored a record of the current BACKUP operation.

Thus, to back-up, for the first time, all the word processor files whose path is \DATA\WPFILES, we type

  C:\>**BACKUP C:\DATA\WPFILES*.* A:**

while to back-up only files modified since they were last backed up, we type

  C:\>**BACKUP C:\DATA\WPFILES*.* A:/M**

In both cases, the wildcard characters *.* ensures that all files with all their extensions in the WPFILES subdirectory are backed up.

The pre-DOS 6 RESTORE external command allows you to de-archive files. It is the only utility which can restore to the hard disc files previously copied to floppy discs using the BACKUP command. The RESTORE command takes the form:

RESTORE *source destination switches*

> where *source* is the drive to restore from,
> *destination* is the drive/path/files to restore, and
> *switches* are:
>
> /a: *date* restores only those files last modified on or after the specified date
>
> /b: *date* restores only those files last modified on or before the specified date
>
> /p to prompt Y/N? before restoring, and
>
> /s to also restore files from subdirectories.

Thus, typing

```
C:\>RESTORE A: C:\DATA\WPFILES\*.*/P
```

restores selected files from the floppy disc in the A: drive to the subdirectory WPFILES in the C: drive, provided these files were backed up from the same named subdirectories.

The PRINT & PRTSC Commands

The first time the PRINT command is used it has to be loaded into memory as it is an external MS-DOS command. However, from then on it resides in memory and can be used without having to re-load it.

The PRINT command provides background printing, that is, it can print long text (or ASCII) files while you are doing something else with your computer. In fact, using this command provides you with a print spooler which allows you to make and control a queue of several files for printing. The command takes the form:

```
C:\>PRINT filespec
```
      adds filespec to print queue

```
C:\>PRINT filespec /C
```
      cancels printing that file

```
C:\>PRINT /T
```
      terminates all printing

```
C:\>PRINT
```
      displays files in queue

The PRINT command assumes that you have continuous paper in your printer. There is no facility to pause printing.

To print the two text files TEXT1.DOC and TEXT2.DOC, type

```
C:\>PRINT TEXT1.DOC
C:\>PRINT TEXT2.DOC
```

Wildcard characters can also be used in the command, as follows:

```
C:\>PRINT TEXT*.DOC
```

which will spool all the files starting with the characters TEXT and having the extension .DOC to the printer.

Text which is displayed on the screen can be sent to the printer by pressing the Print Screen <Shift+PrtSc> key.

On the other hand, pressing the <Ctrl> and <PrtSc> keys simultaneously causes redirection of output to the printer. To cancel the effect, repeat the same key stroke.

Managing Your System

MS-DOS provides several commands which help you to manage and control your system's environment. Some of these commands are internal MS-DOS commands and some are external. First we discuss the internal commands.

Changing the Access Date of a File:

If your computer is not fitted with a battery backed clock and you have not been entering the correct time and date on booting up the system, then all your saved files will be showing the default date 1/1/80 in the directory entry. To change this date for a given file, set the current TIME and DATE and type

```
C:\>COPY filespec + filespec
```

where filespec stands for drive, path, filename and extension. Ignore the message 'Content of destination file lost before copy' given by MS-DOS when this command has been executed.

The SET Command:

To find out what parameters have been set up, type

```
C:\>SET
```

at the prompt, which would evoke a response similar to the following:

```
COMSPEC=C:\COMMAND.COM
PATH=C:\;C:DOS;C:\COMMS
PROMPT=$P$G
```

COMSPEC shows which Command Processor is being used by the system, while PATH and PROMPT display the corresponding commands in your AUTOEXEC.BAT file.

The TYPE Command:

This command allows you to see on screen the contents of text files. The command takes the form:

```
C:\>TYPE filespec
```

The TYPE command is useful because it only lets you have a look at the contents of files without changing the environment in any way. For example, if you ever wanted to find out what is held in either the CONFIG.SYS or AUTOEXEC.BAT files, then use this command rather than the editor; it is much faster.

If the text file you are looking at is longer than one screen full, then use the <Ctrl+S> key sequence (while holding down the key marked <Ctrl>, press the <S> key once) to stop the scrolling of the display. Any key will start the display scrolling again.

Using TYPE on other than ASCII files (such as a .COM or .EXE file) could cause your system to 'hang' as a result of attempting to display certain sequences of machine code that might be contained in the file. If that happens, use the <Ctrl+Alt+Del> key sequence to reboot the system.

In general, to use the TYPE command to see the contents of files, you must be logged into the subdirectory where the file is found or give the full filespec.

For example, to look at the contents of the DOS.BAT file (which is to be found in the BATCH subdirectory) when at the C:\> prompt, you will have to use:

```
C:\>TYPE \BATCH\DOS.BAT
```

The TYPE command could be used to direct text files to the printer by typing

```
C:\>TYPE EXAMPLE.TXT >PRN
```

where PRN stands for 'printer' which is connected to the parallel printer port.

The VER & VOL Commands:

To find out which version of MS-DOS/PC-DOS you are currently using, type

```
C:\>VER
```

at the prompt.

To find out the volume label of the disc in the logged drive, type

```
C:\>VOL
```

at the prompt. If the disc was not labelled during formatting, then the computer will respond with

```
Volume in drive B has no label
```

otherwise the appropriate label will be displayed.

The MORE & SORT Filter Commands:

The TYPE command can be used with a pipe (l) and the MORE external filter command, to view text files one page (23 lines) at a time - after displaying the first page, you are prompted to press a key to display the next page. As such, it can be combined with other commands to control scrolling of long ASCII files. For example,

```
C:\>TYPE EXAMPLE.TXT |MORE
```

or even used by itself (giving quicker response) as

```
C:\>MORE <EXAMPLE.TXT
```

can help you with viewing long text files if you are not used to or quick enough to use the <Ctrl+S> key sequence to halt scrolling, after issuing the TYPE command.

One of the ways in which the DIR command can be used with a pipe (|) and the SORT external filter command, is to sort and display alphabetically the contents of a directory. For example,

```
C:\>DIR |SORT
```

will sort the contents of the logged directory, including the header and footer information, and display the result. For long directories, use this command together with the MORE filter, as follows:

```
C:\>DIR |SORT |MORE
```

to display the sorted directory a page at a time. A hard copy of the sorted directory of a disc could be obtained by typing

```
C:\>DIR |SORT >PRN
```

which redirects output through the parallel printer port.

In fact, sorting directory listings in this way produces a rather jumbled mix of files and subdirectories. A much better way would be with the sort switches of the DIR command. To find out how to use these, type

```
dir /?
```

at the command prompt.

4. THE MS-DOS EDITOR

MS-DOS provides you with a full screen editor, called **Edit**, with which you can create special ASCII files that customise your system. These are text files which, when sent to the screen or printer, are interpreted as text, unlike the .COM or .EXE files which are binary files.

Edit can also be used to create the source code of various programming languages, such as Fortran and C. In such cases, do remember to give the files the appropriate extension, which for the two languages mentioned, are **.for** and **.c**, respectively.

To invoke **Edit**, the disc that contains it must be accessible and the full path of the file you want to create or edit must be specified. Thus, typing the command:

```
C:\>edit test.txt
```

expects to find both **Edit** and the fictitious file **test.txt** on the disc in the logged drive (in this case C:) or on the system PATH, while typing

```
C:\>edit A:test.txt
```

expects to find **Edit** on the C: drive, and the file **test.txt** on the disc in the A: drive.

If the file does not exist on the specified disc or directory, then **Edit** displays a blank screen, as follows:

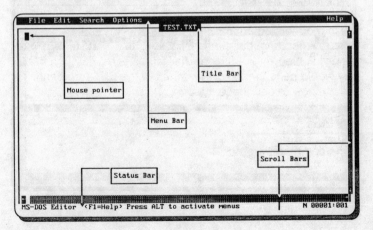

The **Edit** screen is subdivided into several areas which have the following function:

Area	Function
Menu bar	allows you to choose from several main menu options
Title bar	displays the name of the current file. If a new file, it displays the word <Untitled>
Status bar	displays the current file status and information regarding the present process
Scroll bar	allows you to scroll the screen with the use of the mouse.

The area bounded by the Title bar and the two Scroll bars is known as the view window. It is in this area that you enter the contents of a new file or load and view the contents of an old file.

The **Edit** screen can also be invoked from within DOS Shell by selecting the **Editor** from the Main group of programs, as shown below:

On starting **Edit**, the dialogue box shown below appears in the middle of the screen asking you to type in the name of the file you want to edit. Type **test.txt** and either click the <OK> button in the dialogue box, or press the <Enter> key.

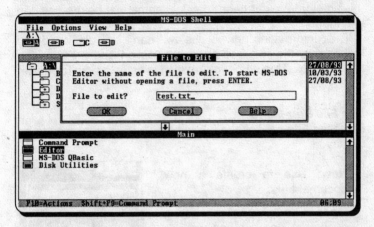

The Editor Menu Bar

Each menu bar option on the editor, has associated with it a pull-down sub-menu. To activate the menu bar, either press the <Alt> key, which causes the first item on the menu bar (in this case **File**) to be highlighted, then use the right and left arrow keys to highlight any of the items of the menu bar, or use the mouse to point to an item. Pressing either the <Enter> key, or the left mouse button, reveals the pull-down sub-menu of the highlighted menu item.

The pull-down sub-menus can also be activated directly by pressing the <Alt> key followed by the first letter of the required menu option. Thus pressing <Alt+O>, causes the **Options** sub-menu to be displayed. Use the up and down arrow keys to move the highlighted bar up and down within a sub-menu, or the right and left arrow keys to move along the options of the menu bar. Pressing the <Enter> key selects the highlighted option, while pressing the <Esc> key closes the menu system.

The Menu Bar Options:

Each item of the menu bar offers the options described below. However, dimmed command names in the **Edit** sub-menu indicate that these commands are unavailable at this time; you might need to select some text before you can use them.

The information given below can be displayed by highlighting the required sub-menu option and pressing the **F1** help key. This same information is listed below for easier reference.

The File Sub-Menu

Selecting **File** causes the following pull-down sub-menu to be displayed:

New: Use to create a new document file.

Open: Use to open an existing document so you can edit or print it.

Save: Use to save the current version of your document.

Save As: Use to save your document as a file. To preserve the previous version of your document, rename it in the File Name dialogue box.

```
┌─────────────────┐
│ File            │
├─────────────────┤
│ New             │
│ Open...         │
│ Save            │
│ Save As...      │
├─────────────────┤
│ Print...        │
├─────────────────┤
│ Exit            │
└─────────────────┘
```

Print: Use to print all or part of a document.

Exit: Use to quit the MS-DOS Editor environment.

The Edit Sub-Menu

Selecting **Edit** causes the following pull-down sub-menu to be displayed:

Cut: Use to remove selected text and put it on the Clipboard, a temporary holding area.

```
┌──────────────────────┐
│ Edit                 │
├──────────────────────┤
│ Cut       Shift+Del  │
│ Copy      Ctrl+Ins   │
│ Paste     Shift+Ins  │
│ Clear          Del   │
└──────────────────────┘
```

62

Copy: Use to copy selected text to the Clipboard. The original text remains unchanged.

Paste: Use to insert a block of text from the Clipboard at any point in a document.

Clear: Use to delete selected text without copying it to the Clipboard. The Clipboard's contents remain unchanged.

The Search Sub-Menu

Selecting **Search** causes the following pull-down sub-menu to be displayed:

Find: Use to search for a text string. You can request a case-sensitive match or a whole-word match.

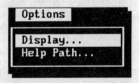

Repeat Last Find: Use to repeat the search performed by the most recent Find or Change command.

Change: Use to replace one text string with another.

The Options Sub-Menu

Selecting **Options** causes the following pull-down sub-menu to be displayed:

Display: Use to control screen colour, scroll bars in windows, and the number of spaces the <Tab> key advances the cursor.

Help Path: Use to change the directories that the MS-DOS Editor searches to find the Help file EDIT.HLP

Help Menu

Selecting **Help** causes the following pull-down sub-menu to be displayed:

Getting Started: Use to find out about using MS-DOS Editor menus, commands, and dialogue boxes. Also to get Help on using the Editor and using options when starting the program.

Keyboard: Use to find out about keystrokes for performing tasks on the MS-DOS Editor, and the WordStar keystrokes that can be used with it.

About: Use to display the version number and copyright information for the MS-DOS Editor.

Dialogue Boxes:

Three periods after a sub-menu option, means that a dialogue box will open when the option is selected. A dialogue box is used for the insertion of additional information, such as the name of a file to be opened, or to be acted upon in some way.

To understand dialogue boxes, type the word 'hi' in the edit screen, then press **Alt+S**, and select the **Change** option from the revealed sub-menu of **Search**. The dialogue box shown below will now appear on the screen.

```
┌──────────────────── Change ────────────────────┐
│                                                 │
│  Find What: ┌─────────────────────────────────┐ │
│             │hi                               │ │
│             └─────────────────────────────────┘ │
│                                                 │
│  Change To: ┌─────────────────────────────────┐ │
│             │hello                            │ │
│             └─────────────────────────────────┘ │
│                                                 │
│                                                 │
│     [ ] Match Upper/Lowercase      [ ] Whole Word │
│                                                 │
│  < Find and Verify > < Change All > < Cancel > < Help > │
│                                                 │
└─────────────────────────────────────────────────┘
```

The <Tab> key can be used to move the cursor from one field to another within a dialogue box, while the <Enter> key is only used to indicate that the options within the various fields within the dialogue box are specified correctly. Every dialogue box contains one field which is enclosed in emboldened angle-brackets (<Find and Verify>, in the above example). This field indicates the action that **Edit** will take if

64

the <Enter> key is pressed (in our example, the word 'hi' will be changed to 'hello', if this is what we choose to type against the 'Find What' and 'Change To' fields. Pressing the <Esc> key aborts the menu option and returns you to the editor.

The cursor can be moved to any part of the text being typed in the view window, and corrections can be made, with the use of the key strokes described below.

Key	Function
←	moves the cursor to the left by one character.
→	moves the cursor to the right by one character.
Ctrl+←	moves the cursor to the beginning of the previous word on the current line.
Ctrl+→	moves the cursor to the beginning of the next word on the current line.
Home	moves the cursor to the first column of the current line.
End	moves the cursor to the end of the last word on the current line.
↑	moves the cursor up one line.
↓	moves the cursor down one line.
Ctrl+Home	moves the cursor to the first line of the current screen.
Ctrl+End	moves the cursor to the last line of the current screen.
PgUp	moves the cursor to the previous screen.
PgDn	moves the cursor to the next screen.

Ctrl+PgUp	moves the cursor left one screen.
Ctrl+PgDn	moves the cursor right one screen.
Ins	toggles the Insert mode from ON (its default position) to OFF and back again.
Enter	moves the cursor to the beginning of the next line, provided the insert mode is in the ON position.
Ctrl+Y	deletes the line at the current cursor position.
Ctrl+N	inserts a blank line at the current cursor position.
Shift+Arrows	(any one of ←↑→↓ arrow keys) marks block areas on the screen to be used with the sub-menu of the Edit option, namely Cut, Copy, Paste, and Clear.

When areas of text are marked, with either the use of the <Shift+Arrows> or by clicking and dragging the mouse, the **Edit**, **Cut** and **Copy** options store the contents of the blocked (highlighted) area of text in a temporary storage area known as the 'Clipboard' from which it can be retrieved later when the **Paste** option is used. The Clipboard stores only one block of information at a time. If you attempt to store a second block of information, it simply overrides the previously stored block.

If you are not using a mouse, you might want to clear the scroll bars from the screen, to give you more room. This can be done by pressing <Alt+O>, selecting the **Display** option and pressing the <Tab> key until the cursor is positioned in the 'Scroll Bars' field. Pressing the spacebar toggles the option into the off position by clearing the letter X from within the square brackets.

If you are using a mouse, scrolling text in the view window is easy. Place the mouse pointer on the top, bottom, left or right of the scroll bars and click the left mouse button to scroll upwards, downwards, to the left or to the right, respectively.

There are a lot more commands associated with **Edit**, but you'll find that the ones given above are sufficient for almost all your needs.

Creating & Saving a Text File

As an example, type the following four lines in **Edit**'s view window, pressing the <Enter> key at the end of each line.

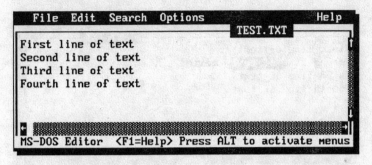

Editing Text:

To edit any part of the document, use the up or down arrow keys to place the cursor at the beginning of the line you want to edit, then use the right or left arrow keys to place the cursor at the required position where you want to begin editing.

If you have a mouse, simply point to the place you want to edit and click the left mouse button to place the cursor at the position occupied by the mouse pointer.

Use one of the above techniques to change the second line of our document to

```
Second line of text, edited
```

Selecting Text:

To select text with the keyboard, place the cursor at the required starting position, and while holding down the <Shift> key, press the right or left arrow keys to highlight as much of the text on that line as you like.

To select text with the mouse, place the mouse pointer at the required starting position and while holding down the left mouse button, move the mouse horizontally to the right or left to highlight the required text on that line. If you try to select text which runs to more than one line, the whole line (first and subsequent) will be selected. Thus, you can either select text from part of a line, or you select text from whole lines.

As an example, select the words ' of text' (including the leading space) from the second line, as shown below:

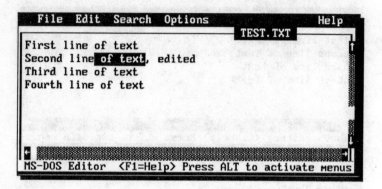

Moving Text:

Having selected the part of text you want to move, use the **Edit, Cut** command, then place the cursor at the required point where you would like to move the text to, and use the **Edit, Paste** command. In our example, move the selected text to the end of the fourth line. The result is shown below:

```
  File  Edit  Search  Options                    Help
┌─────────────────────────── TEST.TXT ──────────────────┐
│ First line of text                                   ↑│
│ Second line, edited                                   │
│ Third line of text                                    │
│ Fourth line of text of text                           │
│                                                       │
│                                                       │
│                                                      ↓│
│                                                       │
 MS-DOS Editor  <F1=Help> Press ALT to activate menus
```

Clearing Text:

To remove text from a document without changing the contents of the Clipboard, highlight the unwanted text, then use the **Edit, Clear** command.

Use this command to remove from the fourth line both repetitions of the words 'of text', then, to prove that the contents of the Clipboard have not changed, use the **Edit, Paste** command to restore the fourth line to its original form.

In fact, you can paste the contents of the Clipboard to any part of a document, as many times as you like, because pasting does not empty the Clipboard.

Copying Text:

To copy text, highlight the required text, then use the **Edit, Copy** command.

Use this command to copy the whole of the second line to the Clipboard, then use the **Edit, Paste** command, to paste a copy of it on to the fifth line of the document. Next, change the words 'Second' to 'Fifth' and 'edited' to 'added', as shown below.

```
 File  Edit  Search  Options              Help
                              TEST.TXT
First line of text
Second line of text, edited
Third line of text
Fourth line of text
Fifth line of text, added




MS-DOS Editor  <F1=Help> Press ALT to activate menus
```

You will have to use the <Del> key to delete the unwanted words as the editor is normally in 'insert' mode and when typing text it inserts it at the cursor position. To toggle the edit mode from 'insert' to 'overtype', press the <Ins> key once.

Finding Text:

To find a specific word or part of a word, use the **Search, Find** command which causes the following dialogue box to appear on your screen:

```
  File  Edit  Search Options                                    Help
 ┌───────────────────────── TEST.TXT ──────────────────────────┐
 │First line of text                                            │
 │Second line of text, edited                                   │
 │Third line of text                                            │
 │Fourth line of text                                           │
 │Fifth line of text, added                                     │
 │        ┌──────────────────── Find ───────────────────┐       │
 │        │                                              │       │
 │        │  Find What:  ┌Fi─────────────────────────┐   │       │
 │        │              └───────────────────────────┘   │       │
 │        │                                              │       │
 │        │    [ ] Match Upper/Lowercase    [ ] Whole Word│      │
 │        │                                              │       │
 │        │   < OK >       < Cancel >      < Help >       │       │
 │        └──────────────────────────────────────────────┘       │
 │                                                              │
 └──────────────────────────────────────────────────────────────┘
 F1=Help   Enter=Execute   Esc=Cancel   Tab=Next Field   Arrow=Next Item
```

Note that the word nearest to the cursor is offered in the 'Find What' field as a default. In the above example, if the cursor is at the beginning of the document, the default word will be 'First'.

As an example, to find all the words that begin with the letters 'Fi', after typing these in the 'Find What' field, press the <**OK**> button. **Edit** highlights the first word containing these letters, and to find the next occurrence you will have to use the **Search, Repeat Last Find** command, or press **F3**.

Saving a Document:

To save a document that you have already named, use the **File, Save** command. To save an unnamed document, or to save it under a different name, use the **File, Save As** command which causes the dialogue box, shown on the next page, to appear on your screen.

70

```
  File  Edit  Search  Options                              Help
┌────────────────────────── TEST.TXT ──────────────────────────┐
│First line of text                                            ▲│
│Second line of tex ┌──────────── Save As ────────────┐        ▓│
│Third line of text │                                 │        ▓│
│Fourth line of tex │ File Name: │TEST.TXT│           │        ▓│
│Fifth line of text │                                 │        ▓│
│                   │ A:\                             │        ▓│
│                   │           Dirs/Drives           │        ▓│
│                   │                                 │        ▓│
│                   │         ┌─────────────┐         │        ▓│
│                   │         │BASIC       ↑│         │        ▓│
│                   │         │COMMS       ▓│         │        ▓│
│                   │         │DATABASE    ▓│         │        ▓│
│                   │         │DOS          │         │        ▓│
│                   │         │SPREADSH     │         │        ▓│
│                   │         │[-A-]        │         │        ▓│
│                   │         │[-B-]       ↓│         │        ▓│
│                   │         └─────────────┘         │        ▓│
│                   │                                 │        ▓│
│                   │  < OK >   < Cancel >   < Help > │        ▼│
│                   └─────────────────────────────────┘         │
└───────────────────────────────────────────────────────────────┘
 F1=Help   Enter=Execute   Esc=Cancel   Tab=Next Field   Arrow=Next Item
```

Note that you can save a document to any subdirectory or drive by selecting appropriately from the Dirs/Drives list within the dialogue box.

Opening a Document:

Once a document has been saved to a file on disc, you can open it by using the **File, Open** command which causes the dialogue box shown below to appear on your screen.

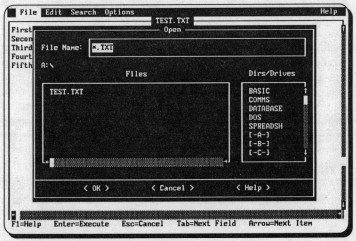

```
  File  Edit  Search  Options                              Help
┌────────────────────────── TEST.TXT ──────────────────────────┐
│First ┌──────────────────── Open ────────────────────┐        ▲│
│Secon │                                              │        ▓│
│Third │ File Name: │*.TXT│                            │        ▓│
│Fourt │                                              │        ▓│
│Fifth │ A:\                                          │        ▓│
│      │          Files              Dirs/Drives      │        ▓│
│      │ ┌────────────────────┐    ┌─────────────┐    │        ▓│
│      │ │TEST.TXT            │    │BASIC       ↑│    │        ▓│
│      │ │                    │    │COMMS       ▓│    │        ▓│
│      │ │                    │    │DATABASE    ▓│    │        ▓│
│      │ │                    │    │DOS          │    │        ▓│
│      │ │                    │    │SPREADSH     │    │        ▓│
│      │ │                    │    │[-A-]        │    │        ▓│
│      │ │                    │    │[-B-]        │    │        ▓│
│      │ │                    │    │[-C-]       ↓│    │        ▓│
│      │ └─┤█├────────────────┘    └─────────────┘    │        ▓│
│      │                                              │        ▓│
│      │   < OK >      < Cancel >      < Help >        │        ▼│
│      └──────────────────────────────────────────────┘         │
└───────────────────────────────────────────────────────────────┘
 F1=Help   Enter=Execute   Esc=Cancel   Tab=Next Field   Arrow=Next Item
```

71

Again, you can select any of the .TXT files (which is the default file extension) from the logged drive and subdirectory, or indeed change the extension to, say, .BAT if you want to work with batch files such as the AUTOEXEC.BAT file. Also note that you can change the logged directory or drive by selecting appropriately from the Dirs/Drives list.

Printing a Document:
To print a document, use the **File, Print** command which causes the following dialogue box to appear on your screen.

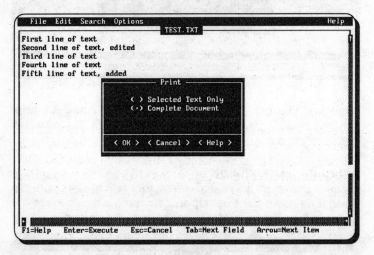

You can choose to print the complete document (the default setting), or a pre-selected part of it. If you are printing the whole document, simply press the <**OK**> button, but if you are printing a selected part of it (which must have been selected before initiating the **File, Print** command), then choose the 'Selected Text Only' option. The **Print** command works only if you have a printer connected to or redirected through your parallel printer port (LPT1).

Exiting the Editor
To end the current session and exit **Edit**, select the **File, Exit** command. If you were working with a file that had not been saved, **Edit** will prompt you to save it before exiting.

72

5. SYSTEM CONFIGURATION

The CONFIG.SYS File

This file allows you to configure your computer to your needs, as commands held in it are executed during booting up the system. The easiest way to amend this system file is with the use of **Edit**, as discussed in the previous chapter.

If you are setting up your system for the first time, and depending on what version of DOS you are using, you might need to change the CONFIG.SYS file that is created for you by the SETUP program, because it might not include all the commands you will require to run your system efficiently. If your system had already been running under an earlier version of DOS, then the SETUP program might have added some extra commands to your CONFIG.SYS file. You might also need to change some of the CONFIG.SYS file commands to optimise your system.

If your system has been implemented by, say, your computer staff, do not edit this file or use **Edit** to look at its contents, unless you have to and you know precisely what you are doing, as the file contains entries that MS-DOS uses to define specific operating attributes. To view the contents of the file, use the **type** command at the system prompt.

DOS Shell =>   To view the contents of a file, select it, then use the **File, View File Contents** command.

Some possible contents of CONFIG.SYS in a pre-DOS 5 version, as well as those for a DOS 5 implementation, are shown on the next page. The list following these two screen dumps, contains commands that you can include within the CONFIG.SYS file. Do look at these, before we discuss how to optimise your system under MS-DOS 6.

However, do remember that any changes made to the CONFIG.SYS file only take effect after you reboot your system, which can be achieved by pressing the 3 keys <Ctrl+Alt+Del> simultaneously.

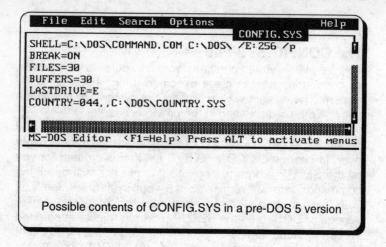

```
 File  Edit  Search  Options                                Help
                                      CONFIG.SYS
SHELL=C:\DOS\COMMAND.COM C:\DOS\ /E:256 /p                      ↑
BREAK=ON
FILES=30
BUFFERS=30
LASTDRIVE=E
COUNTRY=044,,C:\DOS\COUNTRY.SYS

◄ ▓▓▓▓▓▓▓▓▓▓▓▓▓▓▓▓▓▓▓▓▓▓▓▓▓▓▓▓▓▓▓▓▓▓▓▓▓▓▓▓▓▓▓▓▓▓▓▓▓▓▓▓▓▓▓▓▓►
MS-DOS Editor  <F1=Help> Press ALT to activate menus
```

Possible contents of CONFIG.SYS in a pre-DOS 5 version

Under MS-DOS 5 and 6, you can take advantage of high memory to load DOS and some device drivers into it, as follows:

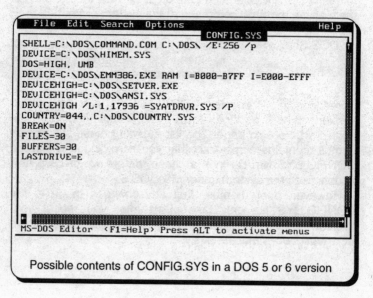

```
 File  Edit  Search  Options                                Help
                                      CONFIG.SYS
SHELL=C:\DOS\COMMAND.COM C:\DOS\ /E:256 /p                      ↑
DEVICE=C:\DOS\HIMEM.SYS
DOS=HIGH, UMB
DEVICE=C:\DOS\EMM386.EXE RAM I=B000-B7FF I=E000-EFFF
DEVICEHIGH=C:\DOS\SETVER.EXE
DEVICEHIGH=C:\DOS\ANSI.SYS
DEVICEHIGH /L:1,17936 =SYATDRVR.SYS /P
COUNTRY=044,,C:\DOS\COUNTRY.SYS
BREAK=ON
FILES=30
BUFFERS=30
LASTDRIVE=E




◄ ▓▓▓▓▓▓▓▓▓▓▓▓▓▓▓▓▓▓▓▓▓▓▓▓▓▓▓▓▓▓▓▓▓▓▓▓▓▓▓▓▓▓▓▓▓▓▓▓▓▓▓▓▓▓▓▓▓►
MS-DOS Editor  <F1=Help> Press ALT to activate menus
```

Possible contents of CONFIG.SYS in a DOS 5 or 6 version

Configuration Commands:

A brief explanation of the configuration commands, which can be included within the CONFIG.SYS file, is given below:

BREAK

By including the command BREAK=ON in the CONFIG.SYS file, you can use the key combination <Ctrl+C> (hold the key marked Ctrl down and press C) or <Ctrl+Break>, to interrupt MS-DOS I/O functions.

BUFFERS

MS-DOS allocates memory space in RAM, called buffers, to store whole sectors of data being read from disc, each of 512 bytes in size. If more data are required, MS-DOS first searches the buffers before searching the disc, which speeds up operations. The number of buffers can be changed by using:

BUFFERS=n

where n can be a number from 1 to 99.

However, as each buffer requires an additional 0.5 Kbyte of RAM, the number you should use is dependent on the relative size between the package you are using and your computer's RAM. Best results are obtained by choosing between 10-30 buffers.

COUNTRY

MS-DOS displays dates according to the US format which is month/day/year. To change this to day/month/year, use the command

COUNTRY=044

where 044 is for U.K. users.

Non U.K. users can substitute their international telephone country code for the 044. The default value is 001, for the USA.

DEVICE

MS-DOS includes its own standard device drivers which allow communication with your keyboard, screen and discs. However, these drivers can be extended to allow other devices to be connected by specifying them in the CONFIG.SYS file. Example of these are:

DEVICE=ANSI.SYS

which loads alternative screen and keyboard drivers for ANSI support - features of which are required by some commercial software.

DEVICE=SETVER.EXE

which sets the MS-DOS version number that MS-DOS versions 5 and 6 reports to a program. You can use the SETVER command at the prompt to display the version table, which lists names of programs and the number of the MS-DOS version with which they are designed to run, or add a program that has not been updated to MS-DOS 5 or 6.

DEVICE=MOUSEAnn.SYS

allows the use of specific mouse devices.

DEVICE=VDISK.SYS n

allows you to specify the size n in Kbytes (default 64) of RAM to be used as an extra very fast virtual disc.

With computers which have more than 640 Kbytes of RAM, the option /E can be used after n in the command to allocate the specified memory size from the extra area of RAM.

DEVICE=DRIVER.SYS

allows you to connect an external disc drive.

DEVICE=EGA.SYS

provides mouse support for EGA modes.

DEVICE=COMn.SYS

specifies asynchronous drivers for the serial ports, where for n=01 specifies an IBM PC AT COM device, and n=02 specifies an IBM PS/2 COM device.

DEVICEHIGH	Loads device drivers into the upper memory area.
DOS	Sets the area of RAM where MS-DOS will be located, and specifies whether to use the upper memory area. The command takes the form:

DOS=HIGH

DRIVPARM	Sets characteristics of a disc drive.
FCBS	Specifies the number of FCBs (File Control Blocks) that can be opened concurrently. The command takes the form:

FCBS=x

where x specifies the total number of files (1-255), that can be opened at any one time (the default value is 4).

FILES	MS-DOS normally allows 8 files to be opened at a time. However, some software such as relational databases, might require to refer to more files at any given time. To accommodate this, MS-DOS allows you to change this default value by using:

FILES=n

where n can be a number from 8 to the maximum required by your application which typically could be 30, although the maximum allowable is 255 (99 in DOS 5).

INCLUDE	New to MS-DOS 6 - it includes the contents of one configuration block within another. This command can be used only within a menu block in your CONFIG.SYS file.

INSTALL	This command runs a terminate-and-stay-resident (TSR) program, such as FASTOPEN, KEYB, NLSFUNC, or SHARE when MS-DOS reads the CONFIG.SYS file. The command takes the following form:

INSTALL=filespec[params]

where *params* specifies the optional line to pass to the *filespec* which must be FASTOPEN.EXE, KEYB.EXE, NLSFUNC.EXE or SHARE.EXE.

LASTDRIVE	This command is used if additional drives are to be connected to your system, or you are sharing a hard disc on a network. The command takes the form:

LASTDRIVE=x

where x is a letter from A to Z (default E).

MENUCOLOR   New to MS-DOS 6 - it sets the text and background colours for the start-up menu. This command can be used only within a menu block in your CONFIG.SYS file.

MENUDEFAULT   New to MS-DOS 6 - it specifies the default menu item on the start-up menu and sets a time-out value. This command can be used only within a menu block in your CONFIG.SYS file.

MENUITEM   New to MS-DOS 6 - it defines up to nine items on the start-up menu. This command can be used only within a menu block in your CONFIG.SYS file.

NUMLOCK   New to MS-DOS 6 - NUMLOCK=OFF (or ON) controls initial setting of the <NumLock> key. This command can only be used within a menu block in your CONFIG.SYS file.

REM   REM followed by any string, allows remarks to be entered in the CONFIG.SYS. A semicolon (;) at the beginning of a line has the same effect.

SET   Displays, sets or removes DOS environment variables. This command can be used in your CONFIG.SYS, your AUTOEXEC.BAT, or at the command prompt.

SHELL	Manufacturers of some micros provide a 'front end' or an alternative Command Processor to COMMAND.COM as real-mode command-line processor. To invoke this, the command SHELL must be included within the CONFIG.SYS file. The command takes the form:

SHELL=FRONTEND.COM

where FRONTEND is the name of the alternative Command Processor. The default value of SHELL is COMMAND.COM.

STACKS	Sets the amount of RAM that MS-DOS reserves for processing hardware interrupts.
SUBMENUU	New to MS-DOS 6 - it defines an item on a start-up menu. This command can be used only within a menu block in your CONFIG.SYS file.
SWITCHES	Specifies the use of conventional keyboard functions even though an enhanced keyboard is installed.
VERIFY	Forces DOS to verify that files are written correctly to disc. The command can also be used at the command prompt.

MS-DOS 6 allows you total control over the execution of your CONFIG.SYS file. For example, pressing **F8** while the boot up message "Starting MS-DOS..." is displayed, permits you to step through the individual lines of the CONFIG.SYS file, answering Yes or No to execute only those commands you require. This makes tracing errors in the start-up routine very simple. Alternatively, pressing **F5** (or the <Shift> key) bypasses both the CONFIG.SYS and AUTOEXEC.BAT files.

For a possible configuration file under MS-DOS 6, refer to the end of this chapter. For multiple configurations, refer to the second half of the next chapter.

The COMMAND.COM Processor:

This command starts a new command processor that contains all internal commands. This is loaded into memory in two parts: the resident part and the transient part which can be overwritten by some programs in which case the resident part can be used to reload the transient part. The command takes the form:

COMMAND [options]

with the following available options:

/E	specifies the environment size in bytes, with a default value of 160 bytes
/P	prohibits COMMAND.COM from exiting to a higher level
/C	executes a following command.

For example, the following statement

```
C:\>COMMAND /C CHKDSK A:
```

which might appear in a program starts a new command processor under the current program, runs the CHKDSK command on the disc in the A: drive, and returns to the first command processor.

The AUTOEXEC.BAT File

This is a special batch file that MS-DOS looks for during the last stages of booting up and if it exists, the commands held in it are executed. One such command is the KEYB xx which configures keyboards for the appropriate national standard, with xx indicating the country. For the U.K., the command becomes KEYB UK, and you will need to execute it if your keyboard is marked with the double quotes sign on the 2 key and/or the @ sign over the single quotes key and/or the £ sign over the 3 key.

The easiest way to amend this system file, as with any text file, is with the use of **Edit**, as discussed earlier.

If you are setting up your system for the first time you might need to change the AUTOEXEC.BAT file that was created for you by the SETUP program, because it might not include all the commands you will require to run your system efficiently. If your system had already been running under an earlier version of DOS, then the SETUP program might have added some extra commands to your AUTOEXEC.BAT file. You might need to change some of the AUTOEXEC.BAT file commands to optimise your system, or to automatically start up an application program or utility.

Some of the possible contents of AUTOEXEC.BAT in a pre-DOS 5 version implementation are shown below.

```
  File   Edit   Search   Options                      Help
                                      AUTOEXEC.BAT
@ECHO OFF
SET COMSPEC=C:\DOS\COMMAND.COM
VERIFY OFF
PATH C:\DOS;C:\WINDOWS;C:\AMIPRO;C:\BATCH
PATH=%PATH%;C:\UTILS;C:\NORTON;C:\NORTON\NBACKUP
SET NBACKUP=C:\NORTON\NBACKUP
C:\WINDOWS\MOUSE
C:\DOS\APPEND \Batch
C:\DOS\KEYB UK,,C:\DOS\KEYBOARD.SYS /ID:166
C:\DOS\GRAPHICS LASERJETII
PROMPT $P$G
SET TEMP=C:\TEMP
SET TMP=C:\TEMP



MS-DOS Editor   <F1=Help> Press ALT to activate menus
```

Possible contents of AUTOEXEC.BAT in a pre-DOS 5 version

Similarly, some of the possible contents of AUTOEXEC.BAT in a DOS 5 implementation, are shown on the next page. In the case of DOS 6, REM out (or delete) the second line of the file, the one starting with SET COMSPEC=; you don't need it.

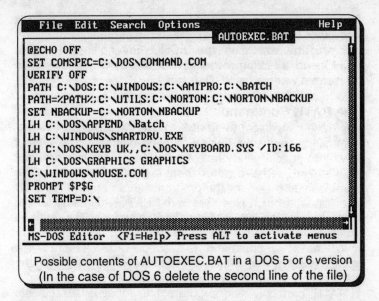

```
  File  Edit  Search  Options                    Help
                              AUTOEXEC.BAT
@ECHO OFF
SET COMSPEC=C:\DOS\COMMAND.COM
VERIFY OFF
PATH C:\DOS;C:\WINDOWS;C:\AMIPRO;C:\BATCH
PATH=%PATH%;C:\UTILS;C:\NORTON;C:\NORTON\NBACKUP
SET NBACKUP=C:\NORTON\NBACKUP
LH C:\DOS\APPEND \Batch
LH C:\WINDOWS\SMARTDRV.EXE
LH C:\DOS\KEYB UK,,C:\DOS\KEYBOARD.SYS /ID:166
LH C:\DOS\GRAPHICS GRAPHICS
C:\WINDOWS\MOUSE.COM
PROMPT $P$G
SET TEMP=D:\



MS-DOS Editor  <F1=Help> Press ALT to activate menus
```

Possible contents of AUTOEXEC.BAT in a DOS 5 or 6 version
(In the case of DOS 6 delete the second line of the file)

Remember that any changes made to the AUTOEXEC.BAT
file only take effect after typing

autoexec

at the system prompt, or after rebooting the system by
pressing the three keys <Ctrl+Alt+Del> simultaneously, or
using the RESET button on your computer.

The list that follows, contains commands that you can
include within the AUTOEXEC.BAT file. Do look at these,
before we discuss how to optimise your system under
MS-DOS 6.

The ECHO Command:

If in your AUTOEXEC.BAT file you do not have the command

    @ECHO OFF

you will notice that every time you boot up the system, the
commands within your AUTOEXEC.BAT file are echoed
(displayed) onto the screen. To avoid such echoes, include
the above command at the beginning of your
AUTOEXEC.BAT file.

Following the echo off command, the path, keyboard, prompt and other commands are executed unseen, until echo is re-activated by executing the ECHO ON command. Using ECHO with a trailing message will display the message on the screen when a batch file is run.

The PATH Command:

It is more convenient to be able to use the MS-DOS external commands from anywhere within the directory tree without having to specify every time where the commands are kept (in our case, we have stored them in the DOS directory). The same could be said for the programs kept in the WINDOWS directory, the batch files kept in the BATCH directory, or the utility programs kept in the UTILS directory. This can be achieved by the use of the PATH command.

Whenever a command is issued, DOS searches the current directory and then all the directories listed on the PATH, for the correct file to execute.

PATH can only find program files, that is, executable command files with the extension .EXE or .COM, or files that DOS recognises as containing such commands, as is the case with .BAT files; for data files you must use the APPEND command as is explained below.

Note the repeated reference to the C: drive within the PATH command, which allows the path to be correctly set even if the user logs onto a drive other than C:.

The APPEND Command:

It is conceivable that the software packages you will be using, require you to type a specific filename in order to activate them. However, some packages also include a second file (most likely a data file which might contain information about the screen display) which is loaded from the first when its name is typed.

In such a case, in addition to including the directory of the package in the PATH command within the AUTOEXEC file to point to the particular package, you must also include the name of the directory within the APPEND command, otherwise MS-DOS will search for the second (data) file in the root directory, as its extension will most likely be .SCR or .OVL and will not search for it down the PATH.

However, if the second file of a package is an executable file (a file with a .EXE or .COM extension), then you must use the /X switch after its name within the APPEND command.

In the display of the last AUTOEXEC file shown previously, the name of the BATCH directory was included in both the PATH and the APPEND command. This allows you to see the contents of a specific batch file, say those of DOS.BAT (to be discussed in the next chapter), by simply typing at the C:\> prompt:

```
TYPE dos.bat
```

If you do not include the BATCH directory in the APPEND command, MS-DOS will not be able to find the file, unless you specify its directory after the TYPE command. Yet when you type at the C:\> prompt:

```
dos
```

MS-DOS searches down the path, finds the file, recognises it as being a file which contains MS-DOS commands (having the .BAT extension), and executes it.

The APPEND command must be included within the AUTOEXEC.BAT file in a position after the PATH command.

Other commands within the AUTOEXEC.BAT file carry out the following functions:

Command	*Function*
VERIFY	Turns ON/OFF verification that files are written correctly to disc.
GRAPHICS	Allows MS-DOS to print on a graphics printer the information appearing on the screen. The parameter GRAPHICS indicates that printer is either an IBM Personal Graphics Printer, an IBM Proprinter, or an IBM Quietwriter printer, while the

	parameter LASERJETII indicates that the printer is an HP LaseJert II. See the Help file for a complete list of supported printers (type Help Graphics).
MOUSE	Loads the mouse driver that comes with the mouse device.
KEYB	Identifies the type of keyboard connected to your system.
PROMPT	Changes the appearance of the MS-DOS command prompt. The parameter $P forces the display of the current drive and path, while the parameter $G displays the greater-than sign (>).
SET	Allows an environment variable named TEMP or TMP to be associated with the string C:\TEMP. This is the subdirectory where Windows application programs create and later deletes temporary files.

A complete summary of all MS-DOS commands is given in the penultimate chapter of this book.

Optimising System Resources

To optimise your system so that resources are used most efficiently, involves choices between providing more memory for the programs you are running and increasing the speed of program execution.

Memory Management in DOS 5 & 6:

On computers with Intel's 80286 or higher processor, MS-DOS 5 or 6 loads itself in 'extended' memory (the memory between 1 and 16 Mbytes - or even higher on 80386 and 80486 machines), freeing at least 45 Kbytes of 'conventional' memory (the first 640 Kbytes of RAM), for your

DOS applications. The extended memory (including the first 64 Kbytes above the 1 Mbyte) known as HMA - the High Memory Area, is managed by HIGHMEM.SYS, while the conventional memory is managed by a built-in memory manager using MCBs (Memory Control Blocks).

A pictorial view of how memory is managed on a typical Intel 80386 or higher processor computer when using MS-DOS 3.3, and what happens when MS-DOS 5 or 6 is used in conjunction with the **DOS=HIGH** command in the CONFIG.SYS file (more about this later), is shown below.

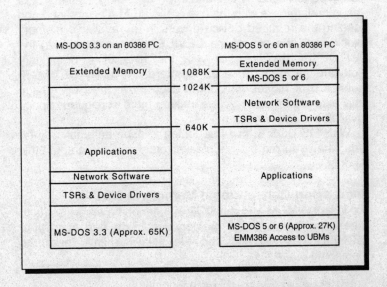

On computers with Intel's less advanced 80286, you can not load device drivers, TSR (Terminate and Stay Resident) programs, and network software drivers into 'upper' memory (the memory between 640 Kbytes and 1024 Mbytes).

The chunks of memory available to the user, between the various hardware-dependent ROMs and the video memory, is managed by UMBs (Upper Memory Blocks) and access to these is governed by the EMM386.EXE utility, thus freeing even more space in conventional memory for DOS applications.

Unfortunately, the 32 Kbyte video ROM splits the free area in upper memory into two sections, a lower area of 32 Kbytes and a higher area of 96 Kbytes. In addition, the 64 Kbyte BIOS ROM sits in the segment just below the 1 Mbyte position. Thus, what you load in upper memory, and where (i.e. in what order), depends on the size of the files you are loading. For this reason, MS-DOS 5 leaves this bit of fine tuning entirely to the user.

The fine tuning of loading the maximum number of device drivers into upper memory when running under MS-DOS 5, can either be done by trial and error, by finding out the size of the various blocks with the use of the **MEM /C** command and loading the required device drivers in the available memory blocks with the use of the **DEVICEHIGH=** command in the AUTOEXEC.BAT file, or with the help of a proprietary software package, such as Quarterdeck's utility QEMM386 version 6 or higher, which can even move the ROM image into extended memory, thus making more contiguous space available in upper memory.

With MS-DOS 6, this fine tuning is done automatically for you when you run the MemMaker program - more about this shortly.

Increasing Conventional Memory in DOS 5:

To install HIMEM and run DOS in extended memory so as to free more conventional memory, use **Edit** and open your CONFIG.SYS file and add the following lines near the beginning of the file:

```
device=c:\dos\himem.sys
dos=high,umb
```

Following the above entries, the optimum order in which your CONFIG.SYS file should start device drivers is:

(a)   the expanded memory manager if the system has actual physical expanded memory,

(b)   the EMM386 device driver which, however, must not be used if you are using an expanded memory manager,

(c)   any device drivers that use extended memory,

(d)   any device drivers that use expanded memory,
(e)   any device drivers that you want to be loaded into high memory using the DEVICEHIGH command.

If you intend to use the EMM386 device driver to provide both expanded memory and to provide access to the unused portions of an 80386 or 80486 processor's upper memory area, use the **ram** switch, as follows:

```
device=c:\dos\emm386.exe ram
```

rather than the **noems** switch, as the latter switch prevents EMM386 from providing expanded memory, but is used to manage the upper memory area only. Although you can specify the size of expanded memory to be provided by including the amount in Kbytes prior to the **ram** switch, this could stop you from running Windows in anything other than real mode. The reason is that EMM386 'converts' the equivalent amount of extended memory to expanded memory and the amount left might not be sufficient to run Windows, which in enhanced mode requires 1,024 Kbytes.

If you are not using a network, set **lastdrive** to E rather than Z, as each letter uses up about 100 bytes more than the preceding one. However, you will not be able to use the **subst** command, which associates a path with a drive letter.

Speeding up Your System:
To speed up program execution, use the **buffers** command in your CONFIG.SYS file to increase the number of buffers (up to 50, depending on the hard disc size) MS-DOS uses for file transfer. The more buffers the faster your system works, but it also uses more memory.

The most effective buffer sizes are: 20 for a hard disc size of less than 40 Mbytes, 30 for a hard disc drive between 40 and 79 Mbytes, 40 for a hard disc drive between 80 and 119 Mbytes, and 50 for hard disc drives in excess of 120 Mbytes. The command takes the form:

```
buffers=40
```

Another way of speeding up your system is to use the SMARTDriVe disc-caching program in your AUTOEXEC.BAT file. An appropriate command might be:

```
c:\dos\smartdrv.exe 1024 128
```

This specifies the cache size should be 1 Mbyte, but will not allow the amount of memory it is using to decrease below 128 Kbytes when Windows requests extra memory to run an application.

The order in which the memory-resident programs were loaded into high memory, is of some importance. The basic principle is that you load the biggest program first, then check using the

```
mem /p
```

command, to find out whether a certain memory-resident program will fit into the available 'gaps'. You might find it useful to use the **lmore** pipe at the end of the **mem** command to stop information from scrolling off your screen.

When MS-DOS encounters the **loadhigh** command, it attempts to load the specified program into the upper memory. However, if the program does not fit into one of the available upper memory blocks, DOS loads it into conventional memory instead. To find out where a particular program has been loaded, use the

```
mem /c |more
```

command.

Issuing this command, causes MS-DOS to display three columns of information; the first column lists the name of the program using your system's memory, the second column gives the size of the program in decimal, while the third column gives the size in hexadecimal. Both the contents of the Conventional Memory and the Upper Memory areas are listed.

If, however, you issue this command while running Windows in enhanced mode (having first shelled out to the DOS prompt before issuing the command), or if you do not include the EMM386 device driver in your CONFIG.SYS file, then the **mem** command will not report the contents of Upper Memory.

A composite screen dump of what you will see on your screen when issuing the **mem /c** command from the DOS system prompt, is shown below:

```
Modules using memory below 1 MB:

Name        Total        =  Conventional  +  Upper Memory
--------    --------        ------------      ------------
MSDOS       14285  (14K)    14285  (14K)           0   (0K)
HIMEM        1168   (1K)     1168   (1K)           0   (0K)
EMM386       3120   (3K)     3120   (3K)           0   (0K)
COMMAND      2912   (3K)     2912   (3K)           0   (0K)
GRAB         8224   (8K)     8224   (8K)           0   (0K)
SETVER        816   (1K)        0   (0K)         816   (1K)
ANSI         4240   (4K)        0   (0K)        4240   (4K)
SVATDRVR     7968   (8K)        0   (0K)        7968   (8K)
APPEND       9040   (9K)        0   (0K)        9040   (9K)
SMARTDRV    28816  (28K)        0   (0K)       28816  (28K)
PORTMGR      4000   (4K)        0   (0K)        4000   (4K)
MOUSE       17088  (17K)        0   (0K)       17088  (17K)
KEYB         6224   (6K)        0   (0K)        6224   (6K)
GRAPHICS     5872   (6K)        0   (0K)        5872   (6K)
Free       732928 (716K)   625408 (611K)      107520 (105K)

Memory Summary:

Type of Memory        Total      =      Used      +      Free
----------------    -----------      -----------      -----------
Conventional        655360  (640K)     29952   (29K)    625408  (611K)
Upper               191584  (187K)     84064   (82K)    107520  (105K)
Adapter RAM/ROM     131072  (128K)    131072  (128K)         0    (0K)
Extended (XMS)     6362016 (6213K)   2319264 (2265K)   4042752 (3948K)
                   -----------      -----------      -----------
Total memory       7340032 (7168K)   2564352 (2504K)   4775680 (4664K)

Total under 1 MB    846944  (827K)    114016  (111K)    732928  (716K)

Largest executable program size      625232  (611K)
Largest free upper memory block       89904   (88K)
MS-DOS is resident in the high memory area.

C:\>
```

If the name of a program or a device driver appears in the Conventional Memory area (apart from MSDOS, HIMEM, EMM386, and COMMAND), then the program or device driver is running in conventional memory, probably because it did not fit into the largest available UMB. This can happen if it is of the type that requires more memory when it is loaded than when it is running, or vice versa. Such a program or device driver might not fit into a UMB even if the size of its file is shown to be less than the largest UMB.

91

If programs do not load in high memory, then you might try including some additional information at the end of the line that loads the EMM386 device driver in your CONFIG.SYS file. This could take the form:

```
i=B000-B7FF i=E000-EFFF
```

which specifically informs the EMM386 memory manager that RAM is available between pairs of addresses (expressed with the i= option). You could also ask the EMM386 memory manager to specifically exclude segments of memory, by using the x= option. However, before you do any of this, install MS-DOS 5 on floppy discs, because if anything goes wrong, you will need a bootable disc to start up your computer.

Each machine has different regions of RAM installed between 640 Kbytes and 1024 Kbytes. For example, on genuine IBM machines, the area of memory between E000-EFFF is the Basic language ROM. Also area C000-C7FF is available, whereas on compatible machines this area is probably not available because of the addressing of various devices such as disc controller firmware. Finally, on *any* machine with a VGA display adaptor, the area of memory used by the CGA system (B000-B7FF) is available to load programs in high memory.

To manage your processor's memory in the most efficient manner, if you are not willing to experiment, you could use one of several proprietary packages, such as Quarterdeck's QEMM386 version 6.01 or higher, which does all this for you automatically.

Using MemMaker in DOS 6

Before you use MemMaker, you should consider how you want to manage your computer's memory. If, for example, you only use Windows applications or run DOS programs from within Windows, then you don't need MemMaker as such Windows applications are not concerned with the amount of available free conventional memory. Furthermore, the DOS applications you run from within Windows will be supplied automatically with all the EMS or XMS memory required.

If, however, you want to run large DOS programs and you also have a number of device drivers and TSRs loaded, then MemMaker comes into its own. It will load automatically for you the maximum number of device drivers into upper memory by typing

```
memmaker
```

at the system prompt. MemMaker displays the following welcome screen.

```
Microsoft MemMaker
_____

Welcome to MemMaker.

MemMaker optimizes your system's memory by moving memory-resident
programs and device drivers into the upper memory area. This
frees conventional memory for use by applications.

After you run MemMaker, your computer's memory will remain
optimized until you add or remove memory-resident programs or
device drivers. For an optimum memory configuration, run MemMaker
again after making any such changes.

MemMaker displays options as highlighted text. (For example, you
can change the "Continue" option below.) To cycle through the
available options, press SPACEBAR. When MemMaker displays the
option you want, press ENTER.

For help while you are running MemMaker, press F1.

                    Continue or Exit? Continue

ENTER=Accept Selection  SPACEBAR=Change Selection  F1=Help  F3=Exit
```

Pressing <Enter> displays a second screen from which you can select either an automatic or custom set-up. We chose the automatic optimisation. MemMaker goes through a process of booting your system and analysing it while doing so, then collects all the information it needs to change your CONFIG.SYS and AUTOEXEC.BAT files. Don't worry, the old ones are saved for you in case you don't like what was done to your system. Finally, MemMaker reboots the system with the new configuration files and displays the results of its efforts, as shown on the next page.

```
Microsoft MemMaker

MemMaker has finished optimizing your system's memory. The following
table summarizes the memory use (in bytes) on your system:

                                      Before        After
        Memory Type                 MemMaker     MemMaker      Change

        Free conventional memory:    619,408      633,872      14,464

        Upper memory:

            Used by programs          77,744       83,968       6,224
            Reserved for Windows           0            0           0
            Reserved for EMS               0            0           0
            Free                     133,760      107,520

        Expanded memory:            Disabled     Disabled


    Your original CONFIG.SYS and AUTOEXEC.BAT files have been saved
    as CONFIG.UMB and AUTOEXEC.UMB.  If MemMaker changed your Windows
    SYSTEM.INI file, the original file was saved as SYSTEM.UMB.

 ENTER=Exit        ESC=Undo changes
```

The configuration file that MemMaker produced for our
80386 system was as follows:

```
 File   Edit   Search   Options                                    Help
┌──────────────────────────────── CONFIG.SYS ─────────────────────────────┐
│ SHELL=C:\DOS\COMMAND.COM C:\DOS\ /E:256 /p                              ↑│
│ DEVICE=C:\DOS\HIMEM.SYS                                                  │
│ DOS=HIGH                                                                 │
│ DOS=UMB                                                                  │
│ DEVICE=C:\DOS\EMM386.EXE NOEMS I=B000-B7FF 2048 I=E000-EFFF              │
│ DEVICEHIGH /L:1,12048 =C:\DOS\SETVER.EXE                                 │
│ DEVICEHIGH /L:1,9072 =C:\DOS\ANSI.SYS                                    │
│ DEVICEHIGH /L:1,17936 =SYATDRVR.SYS /P                                   │
│ COUNTRY=044,,C:\DOS\COUNTRY.SYS                                          │
│ BUFFERS=30,0                                                            │
│ FILES=30                                                                 │
│ LASTDRIVE=E                                                              │
│ FCBS=4                                                                   │
│ BREAK=ON                                                                 │
│                                                                          │
│ ■                                                                       ↓│
 MS-DOS Editor  <F1=Help> Press ALT to activate menus
```

The corresponding AUTOEXEC.BAT file, shown overleaf,
contained the following commands:

94

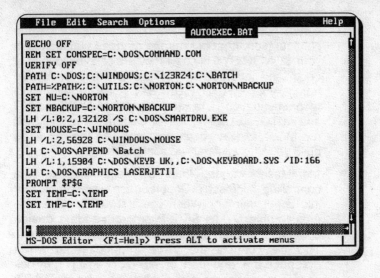

```
 File   Edit   Search   Options                            Help
                        AUTOEXEC.BAT
@ECHO OFF
REM SET COMSPEC=C:\DOS\COMMAND.COM
VERIFY OFF
PATH C:\DOS;C:\WINDOWS;C:\123R24;C:\BATCH
PATH=%PATH%;C:\UTILS;C:\NORTON;C:\NORTON\NBACKUP
SET NU=C:\NORTON
SET NBACKUP=C:\NORTON\NBACKUP
LH /L:0;2,132128 /S C:\DOS\SMARTDRV.EXE
SET MOUSE=C:\WINDOWS
LH /L:2,56928 C:\WINDOWS\MOUSE
LH C:\DOS\APPEND \Batch
LH /L:1,15904 C:\DOS\KEYB UK,,C:\DOS\KEYBOARD.SYS /ID:166
LH C:\DOS\GRAPHICS LASERJETII
PROMPT $P$G
SET TEMP=C:\TEMP
SET TMP=C:\TEMP

MS-DOS Editor   <F1=Help> Press ALT to activate menus
```

In the above AUTOEXEC.BAT file, all the memory-resident
programs, such as **smartdrive**, **mouse**, **append**, **keyb**, and
graphics are loaded into high memory with the **loadhigh**
(you can abbreviate it to **lh**) command, while the **set**
command is used to set the TEMP and TMP environment
variables to C:\TEMP.

Manual Memory Management:
If your device drivers and/or TSRs don't all fit in upper
memory after running MemMaker, then fine-tune your system
manually. Some of the reasons and possible solutions are:

- MemMaker can not load TSRs installed using the
  install command from within the CONFIG.SYS file,
  into upper memory. To load TSRs high you must
  move them into the AUTOEXEC.BAT file and use
  instead the **loadhigh** command.

- MemMaker can not process the contents of batch
  files you execute from the command prompt or you
  jump to from your AUTOEXEC.BAT file. If these batch
  files load TSRs, then edit them by inserting **lh** at the
  start of each line that loads such TSRs.

- MemMaker does not recognise the new menu commands employed within a multiple start-up configuration. It processes the **device=** commands in your CONFIG.SYS file as if they are all to be loaded at once, and ignores the TSRs which may be loaded from your AUTOEXEC.BAT file. Microsoft's recommendation is to create separate CONFIG.SYS and AUTOEXEC.BAT files for each menu option, then run MemMaker on each one, and use the results to build your multiple start-up configuration.

- MemMaker cannot load by itself the software controlling Microsoft's DoubleSpace disc compressor into upper memory. When you first run DoubleSpace (see Chapter 7), its SETUP program adds a **device** command for **dblspace.sys** in your CONFIG.SYS file. This file controls the place in memory to which **dblspace.bin** (the part of MS-DOS which provides access to your compressed drives) is to be moved. To force **dblspace.bin** into upper memory, change this device command to

  devicehigh=c:\dos\dblspace.sys /move

  in your CONFIG.SYS file.

Do remember, however, that if your device drivers and TSRs already fit in upper memory, trying to gain more conventional memory for the sake of it, at the expense of extended memory which can be used for something else (particularly Window applications), is a bad move.

6. CONTROLLING YOUR SYSTEM

The DOSKEY Utility Program

MS-DOS 5 and 6 comes with an external utility called DOSKEY. This utility, when loaded into your system, allows you to recall the most recently entered DOS commands at the system prompt, for subsequent use, which can save you a lot of retyping. You will find that learning to use DOSKEY will be extremely useful to you in what follows in this chapter.

DOSKEY is an example of a special type of program, called TSR (terminate-and-stay-resident). Once a TSR is loaded into memory, it stays in the background without interfering with the other programs you are running. To load DOSKEY into RAM, type

```
DOSKEY
```

at the system prompt and press <Enter>. This causes a message to appear on your screen informing you that the program has been loaded into memory.

If you are going to use DOSKEY frequently, it will be better to include the line

```
C:\DOS\DOSKEY
```

in your AUTOEXEC.BAT file, which loads the program automatically every time you switch on your system.

If you have a computer with an 80386 or higher processor, you should load DOSKEY in the upper memory with the command

```
LH C:\DOS\DOSKEY
```

so as to avoid occupying about 3KB of conventional memory.

Once DOSKEY is in memory, every time you type a command at the system prompt, the command is stored in the DOSKEY buffer which is 512 bytes long. To illustrate how this works, type the following commands, pressing <Enter> at the end of each line:

```
type config.sys
```

and after the contents of the CONFIG.SYS file have been displayed on screen, type

```
type autoexec.bat
```

and after the contents of the AUTOEXEC.BAT file have been displayed, type the commands

```
copy config.sys \batch
copy autoexec.bat \batch
```

The last two commands copy the two precious files into the \BATCH subdirectory, for safety's sake.

To recall the most recently executed DOS command, simply press the <↑> key. Each time this is pressed, the next most recently executed DOS command is displayed. In our case, pressing the <↑> key 4 times, takes us to the first command typed in the above example.

When the required command is displayed at the prompt, pressing the <←> or <→> keys allows you to edit the recalled command, while pressing <Enter> re-executes the chosen command.

The key movements associated with DOSKEY, are as follows:

Key	Result
↑	Displays the previous command in the buffer list.
↓	Displays the next command in the buffer list.
F7	Displays a numbered list of the commands in the buffer.
F8	Cycles through the commands in the buffer that start with a letter you specify.
F9	Prompts you for the number of the stored command in the list (obtained by using the F7 function key).
PgUp	Displays the first command in the buffer list.
PgDn	Displays the last command in the buffer list.
Esc	Clears the command at the prompt.
Alt+F7	Clears the list of commands from the buffer.

Simple Batch Files

To complete the implementation of the hard disc, we need to create a few batch files which we will put in a subdirectory of the root directory, called BATCH. This will help to run the system efficiently. For example, we might require to know the exact name of a DOS or a COMMS command. This can be arranged by creating a batch file for each, to display the corresponding directory whenever the appropriate name is typed. As an example, first create the BATCH subdirectory, using the

```
C:\>MD \BATCH
```

command, then use **Edit** to create the DOS.BAT file in the BATCH subdirectory, as follows:

```
C:\>edit \BATCH\DOS.BAT
```

and type into the editor's screen the following information:

```
@ECHO OFF
CD \DOS
DIR /P
CD \
```

then save the file using the **File, Save** command. In line 2, the directory is changed to that of DOS and line 3 causes the contents of the DOS directory to be displayed using the paging (/P) option. Finally, line 4 returns the system back to the root directory.

However, before you can use the DOS.BAT batch file, you must include the subdirectory BATCH within the PATH command of your AUTOEXEC.BAT file. Having done this, save the changes and reboot the system, so that the latest changes to your AUTOEXEC.BAT file can take effect. Now, typing DOS displays the DOS directory, while typing any external MS-DOS command, invokes the appropriate command. A similar batch file can be built for displaying the COMMS directory, the only difference being in line 2 of the file, so that the correct directory is accessed and displayed.

Using Replaceable Parameters:

After some time has elapsed and you have written several batch files using the

```
C:\>edit \BATCH\MYFILE.BAT
```

command, where MYFILE.BAT is the batch file you are writing, you might find it easier to write a special batch file which itself calls **edit**, tells it into which subdirectory you want it to be created, and also adds the extension .BAT automatically for you. To create this special batch file, use **edit**, as follows:

```
C:\>edit \BATCH\EDITBAT.BAT
```

and type into the editor's screen the following information:

```
@ECHO OFF
EDIT \BATCH\%1.BAT
CD \
```

then save the file as EDITBAT.BAT using the **File, Save** command. Note the variable %1 in line 2 which can take the name of any batch file you might want to create. For example, typing

```
C:\>editbat MYFILE
```

at the prompt, starts executing the commands within the batch file EDITBAT.BAT, but substituting MYFILE for the %1 variable. Thus, line 2 causes entry into **Edit** and tells the editor that you want to create a file in the \BATCH directory, called MYFILE, with the extension .BAT added to it automatically.

As a second example, use the batch file EDITBAT.BAT, created above, to create a new batch file, which we will call ADIR.BAT, as follows:

```
C:\>editbat ADIR
```

and type the following instructions into the editor's screen:

100

Pre-DOS 6 users

```
@ECHO OFF
DIR \%1 |SORT |MORE
```

DOS 6 users

```
@ECHO OFF
DIR \%1 /P /O:GN
```

then use the **File, Save** command to save the file. The DOS
6 version of this batch file requests a directory listing to be
paged (/P), with files displayed in sorted order /O, grouping
directories first (G) and listing by name (N) in alphabetical
order. This gives a better result, as directories are listed first,
not included in the sort, as would be the case with the
pre-DOS 6 version.

You can now use this batch file to display the contents of
any directory listed in alphabetical order of filename, a page
at a time, by simply typing **adir** *directory_name* at the prompt.
For *directory_name* you could type **wp\docs** to have the
contents of the **docs** subdirectory, of the **wp** directory,
displayed.

Special Batch-file Commands
Apart from all the DOS commands, there are some specific
commands which can only be used for batch file processing.
These are:

Command	Action
CALL	Allows you to call one batch file from within another.
CHOICE	Prompts you to make a choice in a batch file, by pressing one of a specified set of keys, thus allowing you to build menus.
ECHO	Enables or disables the screen display of commands executed from within a batch file, or displays the message that follows ECHO.

FOR

Repeats the specified MS-DOS command for each 'variable' in the specified 'set of items'. The general form of the command is:

FOR %%variable IN (set of items) DO *command*

where *command* can include any DOS command or a reference to the %%var. For example,

FOR %%X IN (F.OLD F.NEW) DO TYPE %%X

will display F.OLD followed by F.NEW

GOTO label

Transfers control to the line which contains the specified label. For example,

GOTO end

:end

sends program control to the :end label

IF

Allows conditional command execution. The general form of the command is:

IF [NOT] condition command

where 'condition' can be one of

EXIST filespec
string1==string2
ERRORLEVEL=n

Each of these can be made into a negative condition with the use of the NOT after the IF command.

PAUSE

Suspends execution of the batch file.

REM	Displays comments which follow the REM
SHIFT	Allows batch files to use more than 10 replaceable parameters in batch file processing. An example of this is as follows:

```
:begin
TYPE %1 I MORE
SHIFT
IF EXIST %1 GOTO begin
REM No more files
```

If we call this batch file SHOW.BAT, then we could look at several different files in succession by simply typing

```
SHOW file1 file2 file3
```

as the SHIFT command causes each to be taken in turn.

Combining Batch Files:

After you have created several batch files, one for each application you load onto your hard disc, plus several others to look at file lists in utility subdirectories you will realise that each such batch file takes up 2 or 4 KB of disc space, depending on the cluster size of your hard disc, even though individual batch files might only be a few bytes in size. To remedy this situation, you could combine all your batch files into one batch file, call it LOAD.BAT, thus saving considerable disc space.

It will be assumed here that you have 9 batch files which you would like to combine. These might be BATCH.BAT, DOS.BAT, and NORTON.BAT which produce a listing of the corresponding directories, QA.BAT which loads the Q&A integrated package of word processor and database, QPRO.BAT which loads the Quattro spreadsheet, TURBOC.BAT which loads the Turbo C language, SCALC5.BAT, LOTUS24.BAT and LOTUS34.BAT which load the spreadsheets SuperCalc 5, Lotus 1-2-3 Release 2.4 and Lotus 1-2-3 Release 3.4, respectively.

Before we proceed with the writing of the combined batch file, we shall adapt the SHOW.BAT batch file discussed at the end of the previous section, so that we can obtain a listing on the printer of the contents of all the batch files we intend to combine into one, thus making our job easier. The new version of the SHOW.BAT batch file, which should be placed in the BATCH subdirectory, is given below.

```
@ECHO OFF
CD \BATCH
:begin
ECHO %1.bat
@ECHO OFF
TYPE %1.bat |MORE >PRN
SHIFT
IF EXIST %1.bat GOTO begin
ECHO No more files
```

Thus, to obtain a listing of the batch files of interest, simply type

SHOW batch dos norton qa qpro turboc scalc lotus24 lotus34

and press <Enter>. Note that the SHOW batch file has been written in such a way as not to require the extension .BAT to be included after the entry of each of its substitution parameters.

Now, with the help of the listing of these batch files, you can proceed to write the contents of LOAD.BAT, as follows:

```
@ECHO OFF
IF %1==batch GOTO PL1
IF %1==dos GOTO PL2
IF %1==norton GOTO PL3
IF %1==qa GOTO PL4
IF %1==qpro GOTO PL5
IF %1==turboc GOTO PL6
IF %1==scalc GOTO PL7
IF %1==lotus24 GOTO PL8
IF %1==lotus34 GOTO PL9
GOTO END
```

```
:PL1
@echo off
cd\batch
cls
dir/p
GOTO END
:PL2
@echo off
cd\dos
dir/p
GOTO END
:PL3
@echo off
cd\norton
dir/p
GOTO END
:PL4
@echo off
cd\qa
qa
GOTO END
:PL5
@echo off
cd\qpro
q
GOTO END
:PL6
cd\turboc
tc
GOTO END
:PL7
cd\scalc5
sc5
GOTO END
:PL8
@echo off
cd\123r24
lotus
GOTO END
:PL9
@echo off
```

```
cd\123r34
lotus
:END
cd\
```

In the above batch file, we assume that you will be typing the entries corresponding to the substitution parameters in lower case. For example, typing

LOAD qpro

loads the Quattro Pro package.

If you want to make the batch file respond to both uppercase and lower-case letters, then each line containing the IF statement must be repeated, as shown below:

```
IF %1==qpro GOTO PL1
IF %1==QPRO GOTO PL1
```

and so on.

Adopting the lower-case option only, results in a batch file of 596 bytes, which replaces 9 batch files of 301 bytes of total size. However, by doing so you have saved 16 or 32 KB of disc space, depending on the cluster size of your disc drive, which is a considerable saving.

The CHOICE Command

With MS-DOS 6, you can streamline your batch files with the adoption of the **choice** command. The general form of this command is:

CHOICE [/C[:]keys] [/N] [/S] [/T[:]c,nn] [text]

where **/C[:]keys** specifies allowable keys in the prompt of the command. For example, if the following command is in a batch file

choice /c:bdn

what you will see on the screen is

[B, D, N]?

Adding text to the command, such as

   choice /c:bdn Batch, DOS, or Norton

displays

   Batch, DOS, or Norton [B,D,N]?

on the screen.

   If you don't use the /C switch, **choice** uses YN (for Yes/No) as the default.

   The other command switches have the following meaning:

/N	Causes **choice** not to display the prompt
/S	Causes **choice** to be case sensitive
/T[:]c,nn	Causes **choice** to pause for the specified nn (0-99) seconds, after which it defaults to the specified c character.

As an example, we have rewritten the first part of the LOAD.BAT file, discussed in the previous section, to incorporate the **choice** command, as follows:

```
@ECHO OFF
CLS
ECHO.
ECHO A    Display the BATCH Directory
ECHO B    Display the DOS Directory
ECHO C    Display the NORTON Directory
ECHO.
CHOICE /c:abc Select one -
IF ERRORLEVEL 3 GOTO PL3
IF ERRORLEVEL 2 GOTO PL2
IF ERRORLEVEL 1 GOTO PL1
GOTO END
:PL1
@echo off
cd\batch
cls
dir/p
GOTO END
```

```
:PL2
@echo off
cd\dos
dir/p
GOTO END
:PL3
@echo off
cd\norton
dir/p
GOTO END
:END
cd\
```

Notice that the ERRORLEVEL statements are listed in decreasing order because the statement is true if the parameter returned by **choice** is greater than or equal to the parameter specified in the IF command.

Finally, save this batch file under the filename CHOOSE.BAT.

Multiple Start-up Configurations
Sometimes it is important to switch configuration using a Windows set-up one time, or a Network set-up another time. DOS 6 provides for such eventualities.

At a very basic level, you could choose to load a particular device driver by inserting a question mark immediately before the equals (=) sign in your CONFIG.SYS file, as in

```
devicehigh?=c:\dos\emm386.exe
```

This would prompt you as follows

```
devicehigh=c:\dos\emm386.exe [Y,N]?
```

and the driver will only be loaded if you press the <Y> key.

However, this method of offering different configuration is rather clumsy. A better method is to use the new MENUITEM command. The command takes the form

```
menuitem=label, text
```

where 'label' refers to a block of instructions within the CONFIG.SYS file and 'text' is the wording of the corresponding menu item. In addition, you can have a default menu choice and a time-out so that even if you don't make a choice from the keyboard, the system still starts.

As an example, consider the following configuration file:

```
[menu]
menuitem=bypass, Clean boot
menuitem=windows, Load Windows
menuitem=network, Connect to Network

menudefault=network,10

[bypass]

[windows]

[network]
DEVICEhigh=C:\NFS\PCNFS.SYS
DEVICEhigh=C:\NFS\SOCKDRV.SYS
DEVICE=C:\NFS\PKTD.SYS
STACKS=0,0

[common]
SHELL=C:\DOS\COMMAND.COM C:\DOS\ /E:256 /P
COUNTRY=044,,C:\DOS\COUNTRY.SYS
DEVICE=C:\DOS\HIMEM.SYS
DEVICE=C:\DOS\EMM386.EXE noems RAM
x=B000-B7FF I=c800-EFFF frame=e000
DOS=HIGH,UMB
BREAK=ON
FILES=40
BUFFERS=40
LASTDRIVE=V
DEVICEhigh=C:\DOS\ANSI.SYS
DEVICEHIGH=C:\DOS\DBLSPACE.SYS /MOVE
DEVICEhigh=C:\DOS\SETVER.EXE
```

The **menudefault** command specifies the option that will be selected if you press the <Enter> key or after the time set (in seconds) expires.

The rest of the CONFIG.SYS file is divided into blocks of commands headed by a block label, which corresponds to the first parameter of each **menuitem** command. The commands in these configuration blocks are only executed if you select the corresponding option, but you also have the ability to specify a 'common' block for commands you would like executed, irrespective of the chosen configuration.

It is a good idea to include a 'common' block at the end of a multi-configuration file, as this not only stops command duplication, but also stops possible confusion of programs that change your CONFIG.SYS file.

When a choice is made from a start-up menu, DOS automatically sets the CONFIG environment variable with the label corresponding to the selection made. This allows you to also control your AUTOEXEC.BAT file, as the following example shows:

```
@ECHO OFF
VERIFY OFF
PATH C:\DOS;C:\BATCH;C:\UTILS;C:\NORTON
LH KEYB UK,,C:\DOS\KEYBOARD.SYS /ID:166
LOADHIGH MOUSE
MODE co80
SET TEMP=C:\TEMP
SET TMP=C:\TEMP
GOTO %CONFIG%

:bypass
GOTO end

:windows
PATH=%PATH%;C:\WINDOWS;C:\AMIPRO;c:\nfs
SMARTDRV 4096
LH APPEND \Batch
LH GRAPHICS deskjet
LH DOSKEY
win
GOTO end
```

```
:network
PATH=%PATH%;C:\NFS
SET NFSPATH=C:\NFS
SET NFSDRIVE=C:
SET TZ=GMT-1
LH APPEND \Batch
LH GRAPHICS deskjet
LH DOSKEY
LH ne2000 0x66 0x0a 0x0300
LH prt *
NET init
LH r:\llcpkt
LH listener -p 0 -b
rsh csm mail
GOTO end

:end
ECHO H E L L O ... This is Noel's PC using
PROMPT %config% $P$G
VER
```

Note the similar blocks of commands within this AUTOEXEC.BAT, each preceded by a label corresponding to the menu selection within the CONFIG.SYS file. The first GOTO statement diverts program flow to the appropriate label, depending on the value of the CONFIG variable.

On booting your computer, the following display appears on your screen:

```
MS-DOS 6 Startup Menu

   1. Clean boot
   2. Load Windows
   3. Connect to Network

Enter a choice: 3      Time remaining: 09




F5=Bypass startup files     F8=Confirm each CONFIG.SYS line [N]
```

If you intend to optimise the above two files using **MemMaker**, you must split them up and make a number of conventional CONFIG.SYS and AUTOEXEC.BAT files to represent each provided option. Then, optimise these individually using **MemMaker**, and finally build the multiple configuration files from the individual results. **MemMaker** does not work on multiple configuration files, and attempting to use it will only cause major problems. So, be very careful!

Stopping Batch File Execution

To stop a batch file before all its statements and commands have been executed, press the two key combination

```
Ctrl+C
```

or

```
Ctrl+Break
```

more than once, if necessary. DOS displays a message asking you if you really want to terminate the batch file. Typing **Y** (for yes), terminates batch file execution.

Ctrl+C and Ctrl+Break Differences:

The main difference between <Ctrl+C> and <Ctrl+Break> is that the former is recognised and acted upon by the resident part of DOS, while the latter is handled by the BIOS. The BIOS also handles directly the <SysReq>, <Ctrl+Alt+Del>, and <Print Screen> commands. However, the <Ctrl+Break> command can only be effective if BREAK has been switched on from within your CONFIG.SYS file, which can marginally slow down the performance of machines with a less powerful processor than an 80386.

Normally, when you press a key, the BIOS generates a hardware interrupt and leaves it up to DOS to handle it. DOS, in turn, places each keystroke or command (which it interprets as characters) into a queue and passes each one to the appropriate program or the COMMAND processor.

Thus, pressing <Ctrl+C> causes the BIOS to pass the command to DOS to be dealt with when DOS is able to do so, whether BREAK is on or not. However, for <Ctrl+C> to work, it must be the first, or only, command left in the buffer.

In addition, the hardware interrupts must not have been switched off by the running program, otherwise DOS would not have been aware that the command had been issued. To overcome this, press <Ctrl+C> a few times in rapid succession to ensure that DOS is listening and that it is the first one in the buffer.

Pausing a Batch File:

If you would like to temporarily stop a batch file, then either press

`Ctrl+S`

or the

PAUSE

key. This 'freezes' the screen until you press another key.

* * *

MS-DOS has many more commands which can be used to control a micro in special ways. However, this is an area which lies outside the scope of this book. What was covered here, together with the summary of the DOS commands given in the penultimate section of this book, is more than enough to allow effective control of a microcomputer.

If you would like to be able to write customised batch files, create specialist programs with the use of the **debug** program and learn how to design your own professional looking menu screens, then may we suggest that you refer to either the book entitled *A Concise Advanced User's Guide to MS-DOS* (BP264), or the book entitled *Making MS-DOS Work For You* (BP319) also published by Bernard Babani (publishing) Ltd.

* * *

7. MS-DOS 6 UTILITIES

Microsoft have gone to town with version 6 of DOS and have included an excellent range of system utilities, many of which they have 'bought in' from other software houses.

Utilities are included for disc compression and defragmentation, backing up and restoring data, virus protection of your system and for three levels of file-delete protection. These all seem to do a good job, even though some of them are cut-down versions of products sold under their own names.

If we have a criticism, it is that these utilities have not been fully integrated into the package as a whole. They each, for example, have their own inconsistent help systems. Only a minor problem which will probably be addressed by Microsoft before the next release!

Disc Compression

Microsoft's own version of built-in disk compression, **DoubleSpace**, was first included with MS-DOS 6.0. The answer to most Windows users' prayers - the ability to 'double' the storage capacity of your discs with no extra hardware cost. We have tried it, and very successfully, but be aware that some users have had apparent lost data problems as a result of using DoubleSpace compression. The choice of whether to use it is yours. If your life depends on the absolute integrity of your data, maybe you should think twice about using new software that has complete control of it. Version 6.2 includes DoubleGuard, an automatic safety feature which checks the data integrity before writing to a compressed drive. If problems are encountered, your computer is immediately shut down.

How it Works:

Once DoubleSpace is installed on your system it compresses your files in a drive by a default factor of between 1.5 and 2 and hence lets you store much more on that drive. When you use files on a compressed drive DoubleSpace transparently uncompresses them, so that they can be accessed; and then re-compresses them when they are saved.

The decompression and compression of files is carried on automatically in the background. We could not detect any degradation in operating speed, provided the compression rate was not set too high, except when moving files from one compressed drive to another. If you need to do that, we suggest you make a cup of coffee.

When DoubleSpace first compresses a drive it sets up a hidden file on an uncompressed part of the drive which is then treated as a new logical drive. Thus for every hard drive you compress you acquire another drive letter. DoubleSpace skips the first four available drive letters and assigns the next available one to the new drive. For example, if your computer has drives A:, B:, and C:, DoubleSpace skips letters D, E, F, and G, and assigns drive letter H to the new drive, when it compresses the hard disc drive C:. If you compress another fixed drive, DoubleSpace works backwards from the first drive letter it assigned. In the example above, DoubleSpace would next assign the drive letter G.

Once installed DoubleSpace works at the device driver level on your system. When you switch on your computer the file DBLSPACE.BIN is loaded into memory and your disc(s) are compressed, before the commands in your CONFIG.SYS and AUTOEXEC.BAT files are executed. Thus DBLSPACE.BIN is always first loaded into conventional memory, (the lower 640KB of your RAM) since it loads before the device drivers that provide access to your upper memory. This uses over 40 KB of RAM memory which is no longer available to run other application programs. You should also place the device driver DBLSPACE.SYS in your CONFIG.SYS file, with the following statement:

```
DEVICEHIGH=C:\DOS\DBLSPACE.SYS /MOVE
```

Assuming of course that the driver is stored in the C:\DOS directory, if not you should adjust the path statement. The DBLSPACE.SYS device driver does not provide access to compressed drives; it simply determines the final location of DBLSPACE.BIN in memory. When loaded with a DEVICEHIGH command, as above, the DBLSPACE.SYS driver moves DBLSPACE.BIN from conventional to upper memory, if room is available there.

Compressing a Fixed Drive:

As an example, we will step through the procedure of compressing the fixed drive D: on one of our systems. This is in fact an empty 100MB hard card and is one of two mounted in the computer.

There are two ways to use DoubleSpace; from the command line, by using the DBLSPACE command with a series of switches (described briefly later), or more easily, from the front-end program described next. To activate this simply type

    DBLSPACE

When used for the first time this opens the following screen.

```
Microsoft DoubleSpace Setup
═══════════════════════════

        Welcome to DoubleSpace Setup.
        The Setup program for DoubleSpace frees space on your hard
        disk by compressing the existing files on the disk. Setup
        also loads DBLSPACE.BIN, the portion of MS-DOS that provides
        access to DoubleSpace compressed drives. DBLSPACE.BIN
        requires about 40K of memory.

        If you use a network, then before installing DoubleSpace,
        start the network and connect to any drives you normally use.

          o To set up DoubleSpace now, press ENTER.

          o To learn more about DoubleSpace Setup, press F1.

          o To quit Setup without installing DoubleSpace, press F3.




    ENTER=Continue  F1=Help  F3=Exit
```

Press F3 to abort, or <Enter> to open the next screen, shown on the next page. This suggests two ways to install DoubleSpace. You can use **Express Setup** to automatically compress your C: drive, but we do not recommend this. Better to use **Custom Setup**, as described shortly. With Express Setup there is the danger that all your DOS files will be included in the compressed drive and if this is ever accidentally deleted your system will be paralysed.

117

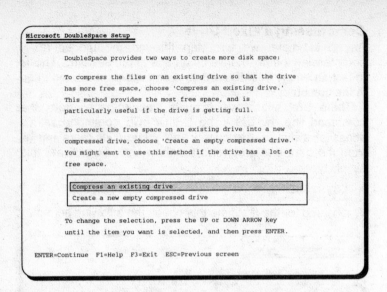

```
Microsoft DoubleSpace Setup

        DoubleSpace provides two ways to create more disk space:

        To compress the files on an existing drive so that the drive
        has more free space, choose 'Compress an existing drive.'
        This method provides the most free space, and is
        particularly useful if the drive is getting full.

        To convert the free space on an existing drive into a new
        compressed drive, choose 'Create an empty compressed drive.'
        You might want to use this method if the drive has a lot of
        free space.

        ┌──────────────────────────────────────────────────────────┐
        │ Compress an existing drive                                 │
        │ Create a new empty compressed drive                        │
        └──────────────────────────────────────────────────────────┘

        To change the selection, press the UP or DOWN ARROW key
        until the item you want is selected, and then press ENTER.

  ENTER=Continue  F1=Help  F3=Exit  ESC=Previous screen
```

If you only have one hard disc, DoubleSpace the free space
on it as drive D:, leaving the C: drive to hold your DOS files,
Windows swap file, etc. If drive D: is not very large, move
files from the C: drive to it, and then increase its size.

Choosing the default option, displays the following screen:

```
Microsoft DoubleSpace Setup

        Select the drive you want to compress:

                       Current         Projected
           Drive      Free Space      Free Space

        ┌──────────────────────────────────────────────────────────┐
        │    C         44.8 MB         160.5 MB                      │
        │    D         99.9 MB         199.8 MB                      │
        │    E         72.9 MB         189.1 MB                      │
        │    F         49.6 MB          99.2 MB                      │
        └──────────────────────────────────────────────────────────┘

        To accept the current selection, press ENTER.

        To select a different drive, press the UP ARROW or DOWN
        ARROW key until the drive you want is selected, and then
        press ENTER. If there are more drives than fit in the
        window, you can scroll the list by pressing the UP ARROW
        DOWN ARROW, PAGE UP, or PAGE DOWN key.

  ENTER=Continue  F1=Help  F3=Exit  ESC=Previous screen
```

In this case, drive D:, the one we have selected to compress, has 99.9MB of free space. When this is accepted the 'C' key is pressed to start the compression process. CHKDISK (or SCANDISK with version 6.2) is run on the drive to be compressed and the computer is rebooted to allow the file DBLSPACE.BIN, which controls the whole compression operation, to load. Make sure that you do not leave any floppy discs in your drives. The system is verified and the actual compression then takes place, as shown below.

```
Microsoft DoubleSpace Setup
═══════════════════════════

        DoubleSpace is now compressing drive D.

        Start time:              20:42:06
        Current time:            20:42:06
        Estimated finish time:   20:43

        Time left:               About 1 minute.

        Currently Compressing:

        ┌─────────────────────────────────────────┐
        │              0% complete                 │
        └─────────────────────────────────────────┘




Creating compressed drive...
```

The new drive is then 'defragmented' to optimise its performance. This entails rebuilding any contained files so that they occupy contiguous space on the disc. In our case this only took a few seconds, as the disc was empty. After a further resizing and system examination a report like the one shown on the next page is produced.

Pressing <Enter> at this stage will again restart your computer, this is necessary to activate the command line

```
DEVICE=C:\DOS\DBLSPACE.SYS /MOVE
```

which is added to the CONFIG.SYS file. If you are using High Memory you should use the DOS editor to change the word DEVICE to DEVICEHIGH in this line, as discussed earlier.

```
Microsoft DoubleSpace Setup
━━━━━━━━━━━━━━━━━━━━━━━━━━━━━━━━━━

        DoubleSpace has finished compressing drive D.

            Free space before compression:    99.9 MB
            Free space after compression:    194.9 MB
            Compression ratio:                2.0 to 1
            Total time to compress:           3 minutes.

        DoubleSpace has created a new drive K that contains 2.0 MB
        of uncompressed space. This space has been set aside for
        files that must remain uncompressed.

        To exit from DoubleSpace and restart your computer, press
        ENTER.




ENTER=Continue
```

The two hidden system files DBLSPACE.BIN and DBLSPACE.INI will also have been added to the root directory of your C: drive. The switch /MOVE, in the above command, moves DBLSPACE.BIN to its final location in memory.

The new drive formed in the above case was K:. Using the DIR command throws some light on the nature of this drive.

```
C:\>dir k:
 Volume in drive K is HOST_FOR_D
 Volume Serial Number is 1ACF-94AE
 Directory of K:\
File not found
```

Drive K: is the host drive for drive D:. In fact drive K: will hold all the compressed files that 'appear' to be in D: in the file DBLSPACE.000. No file was found above because its attributes have been set to SYSTEM, HIDDEN, READ ONLY, as shown by the ATTRIB command:

```
C:\>attrib K:\dblspace.000
    SHR      K:\DBLSPACE.000
```

In our case the actual size of the file DBLSPACE.000 was 102,644,736 bytes, or some 2MB short of the actual size of the whole disc.

DoubleSpace thus hides the compacted file away for safety and lets you use the 'virtual' drive D:. It should not need saying that you should never delete, or tamper with, this file if you want to keep your compressed files intact.

Further Use of DoubleSpace:

The next time you use the **DBLSPACE** command, the system will be scanned and a screen similar to the following will be opened.

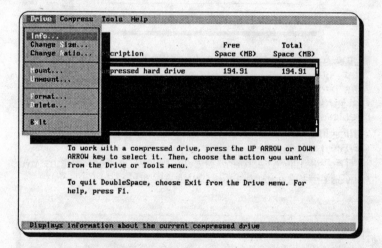

This lists any compressed drives, in our case, just the D: drive and has a menu bar along the top. The **Drive** menu options are displayed above. To see brief details of each menu item, first highlight it and then read the one line help statement at the bottom of the screen. For more detail use the adequate **Help** menu options.

Compressing a Floppy Disc:

As an example of how to use the DoubleSpace front-end, we will step through the operation of compressing a floppy disc. Unfortunately you cannot do this until at least one fixed drive has been compressed. Also you cannot compress a 360KB disc, or one that is already full.

Place an empty and formatted disc in your A drive and select the **Compress**, **Existing Drive** menu option. This opens a list of all the drives in your system that can be compressed, as shown below.

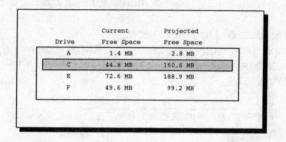

Drive	Current Free Space	Projected Free Space
A	1.4 MB	2.8 MB
C	44.8 MB	160.6 MB
E	72.6 MB	188.9 MB
F	49.6 MB	99.2 MB

If the A: drive does not appear in the list make sure the disc you put in it is not full, not previously compressed and that it has been formatted. In our case above, the D: drive is no longer shown, as it is now compressed. Press <Enter> with the A: drive option highlighted and step through the same procedure as before. It will take about one minute with an empty 1.44MB disc.

The resulting screen, shown below, indicates that two drives are now compressed, both A: and D:.

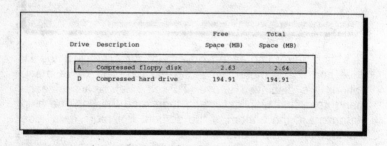

Drive	Description	Free Space (MB)	Total Space (MB)
A	Compressed floppy disk	2.63	2.64
D	Compressed hard drive	194.91	194.91

In these examples we have compressed empty drives, but the system works equally well, albeit much slower, on partially full ones. You cannot compress a full drive though. You leave DoubleSpace with the **Drive**, **Exit** command.

Mounting Floppy Drives:

When you leave DoubleSpace the compressed floppy disc is 'mounted' while it remains in the drive bay. In this state you can save and retrieve files to and from it as normal. However it 'unmounts' when you remove it from the bay and with version 6.0 is then unusable until you mount it again. To demonstrate this, while your newly compressed and empty disc is still mounted in the drive, issue the following DOS command

```
C:\>dir a:
Volume in drive A has no label
Volume  Serial Number is 0DE0-1B51
Directory of A:\

File not found
```

Now unmount the drive from the DOS command line as follows and again use **DIR** to see the discs contents.

```
C:\>dblspace a: /unmount
DoubleSpace has unmounted drive A.

C:\>dir a:
Volume in drive A has no label
Volume Serial Number is 1DE0-1B51
Directory of A:\

READTHIS TXT        350 02/10/93    14:32
 1 file(s)        350 bytes
  2760704 bytes free
```

With **MS-DOS 6.0**, the above display indicates that the disc is compressed and cannot be used until you remount it, either by issuing the DOS command while logged onto the drive, or from the front-end (opened with the **DBLSPACE** command) by using the **Drive**, **Mount** menu command.

This mounting procedure with version 6.0 is a bit of a bore, to say the least. It is especially irritating if you are using several compressed floppy discs in Windows. Every time you change one you have to exit Windows to carry out the mounting procedure, as you cannot run DoubleSpace while Windows is active.

With **MS-DOS 6.2**, and as long as the Automount feature is not disabled, the mounting procedure is fully automatic, even when using Mocrosoft Windows. However, you still cannot access the files on a compressed floppy disc if you use a computer that does not have DoubleSpace running on it.

Using the Command Line:

If you add switches or parameters to the DBLSPACE command, DOS carries out the requested task without starting the DoubleSpace front-end program. The command syntax differs from task to task. A brief description of each main switch is given here, but for more detail, access the MS-DOS Help system.

Each one of the listed switches has its own Help screens, which you can open from the main DoubleSpace help screen. They are used as follows:

```
DBLSPACE /SWITCH
```

but with 'SWITCH' substituted from the list below.

/CHKDSK	Checks the validity of a compressed drive's internal file structure.
/COMPRESS	Compresses a hard disk drive or floppy disk.
/CREATE	Creates a new compressed drive in the free space on an existing drive.
/DEFRAGMENT	Defragments a compressed drive.
/DELETE	Deletes a compressed drive.

/FORMAT	Formats a compressed drive.
/INFO	Displays information about a compressed drive.
/LIST	Displays a list of the drives on your computer. It includes compressed and uncompressed hard disk drives, floppy drives, and other removable drives, but **not** network drives.
/MOUNT	Mounts a compressed volume file (CVF in Microsoft jargon) on a removable drive, so that you can then use the files it contains.
/UNMOUNT	Unmounts a compressed drive.
/RATIO	Changes the estimated compression ratio of a compressed drive.
/SIZE	Changes the size of a compressed drive.

Removing DoubleSpaced Drives:

If at any time you want to return your system to the state it was before you compressed your drives, the procedure is safe and easy. The important thing is first to copy any files you do not want to lose to a safe location. If you don't have space on another hard drive you could back them up to floppy discs, as described in the next section.

Once you are happy that all your files are safe, enter the **Dblspace** command followed by the **Disc**, **Delete** menu commands. Select the compressed drive to delete and press <Enter>. This deletes the selected drive and erases the associated compressed volume file. In other words it erases the entire drive and all the files it contains, so use the action carefully.

If you only want to empty a compressed drive and not remove the drive itself you use the **Drive**, **Format** menu command instead.

Both of these actions can be carried out more quickly (but until you know what you are doing, less safely) by issuing the command at the DOS prompt. For example:

```
DBLSPACE /DELETE D:
```

would delete the compressed drive D: and all its contents, whereas

```
DBLSPACE /FORMAT D:
```

would delete all the contents of compressed drive D:.

With **MS-DOS 6.0**, to remove all traces of DoubleSpace compression from your system, first delete all the compressed drives, as described above. Next change to the root directory of your C: drive and then delete the two files DBLSPACE.BIN and DBLSPACE.INI. As these are protected files, you will have to change their attributes before attempting to delete them (unless you are using a utility like Norton Commander). To do this use the following commands, one at a time

```
ATTRIB -S -H -R C:\DBLSPACE.BIN
DEL C:\DBLSPACE.BIN

ATTRIB -S -H -R C:\DBLSPACE.INI
DEL C:\DBLSPACE.INI
```

We are certainly not recommending that you should carry out the above procedure, but if, after experimenting with disc compression, you decide that it is not for you, you should now be in a position to wipe out all traces of its existence from your computer.

With **MS-DOS 6.2**, you don't have to go through the above process to remove DoubleSpace compression. If you need to uncompress a drive, simply use the **Tools, Uncompress** command from the DoubleSpace screen. However, you can only carry out this procedure, if there is enough room on the disc to hold the files when they are uncompressed.

If you uncompress all the compressed drives on a system, the DoubleSpace driver is removed from the disc and from the memory. You will then have to reinstall DoubleSpace to use it again.

The MSBACKUP Utility

The inclusion of a good backup program is another of the main improvements that DOS 6 has over DOS 5. MSBACKUP comes in two versions, one for DOS and the other to work in the Windows environment. Both are infinitely better than the separate Backup and Restore utilities shipped with DOS 5. A graphical front-end controls all the functions once the program is started. By default backed up files are compressed and although you can turn this feature off, you cannot optimise a backup.

The compression ratio depends on the type of files being handled. With ordinary binary program files a ratio of about 1.4:1 seems the norm, but our word processor files, with included graphics, compress at ratios nearer to 8:1. We have managed to backup a 17MB subdirectory onto only two 1.44MB floppy discs and in only a few minutes as well!

Configuring your System:

To run the utility, type **MSBACKUP** at the DOS prompt. If nothing happens you probably made a poor selection when installing DOS 6, in which case the DOS version of the files will not be in your DOS directory. Not the end of the world, as long as you have the original discs handy. You need to place each of the set-up discs into your A: drive and issue the following command

```
copy A:\msb*.* C:\DOS
```

This will copy all nine of the MSBACKUP files into your DOS directory (obviously if your DOS files are stored somewhere else you will need to amend the above path). There is still more though, three of the files are compacted and will need expanding before they can be used. Change to the DOS directory and issue the following commands

```
expand MSBACKUP.EX_ MSBACKUP.EXE
expand MSBACKUP.HL_ MSBACKUP.HLP
expand MSBCONFG.HL_ MSBCONFG.HLP
del MSB*.*_
```

Be very careful in the last command not to omit the '_' character at the end, otherwise you will delete all the files you have just copied and expanded.

If you plan to use the Backup utility often (which we strongly recommend) you should open a special directory for it to store the many set-up and catalogue files it produces. If you don't do this the DOS directory soon fills up with these files.

Before using MSBACKUP carry out the following two steps. At the DOS prompt type

```
md C:\BACKUP
```

Then enter the following line into your AUTOEXEC.BAT file with your editor

```
set msdosdata=C:\BACKUP
```

This sets a DOS environmental variable which will tell the MSBACKUP program where to find its configuration files, each time it starts up. Restart your computer to make the instruction immediately effective.

The first time you run MSBACKUP you get an 'Alert' message saying that Backup needs configuration. Press <Enter> to start the process, which only takes about five minutes. Accept all the default video and mouse defaults, unless of course your system is non standard, in which case you will almost certainly know about it by now.

Your floppy and hard disc drives are tested and configured next, as is your main processor. You are then faced with the Configure dialogue box, an example of which is shown below:

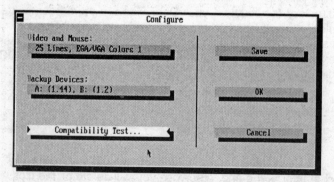

Run the **Compatibility Test** from this box, which carries out a small trial Backup and Compare operation to test the system. You will need two similar and numbered floppy discs. Once you start this test, a macro takes over which gives a rapid overview of the flavour of the program. You will be prompted if you need to do anything, so don't go away.

What you are actually running is a version of Norton Backup, produced by Symantec Corporation. When a new disc is required the computer will ping and a prompt message will appear on the screen, but the disc drive light will not go out. With Norton's Backup you change discs 'on the fly', which in a long operation saves a considerable amount of time. We are assured that this does no harm to the discs, or the drives.

When the configuration is complete a report is generated and hopefully your system will be passed as 100% suitable for future backups.

Backing Up:

We will now step through an actual backup and restore sequence to show how easy the procedures are. Issue the **MSBACKUP** command from the DOS prompt and select **Backup** from the opening dialogue box. This will open the colourful control screen shown below.

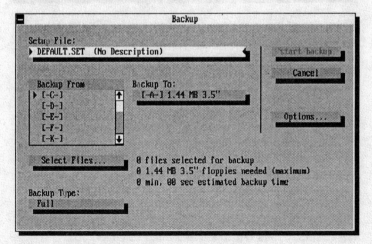

From this box you set all the backup options, select files to backup and choose the destination for the backup. Don't worry about the **Setup File** option, we will discuss it later.

Select the C: drive in the **Backup From** list box and press the **Select Files** button below it. The program will then scan the whole of your C: drive and open a graphical selection screen, like the one shown here.

```
┌─────────────────────────────────────────────────────────────────┐
│ ▄                    Select Backup Files                          │
│ [-C-]  [-D-]  [-E-]  [-F-]  [-X-]                                 │
│                                                                   │
│ C:\DOS\*.*                                                        │
│                                                                   │
│  ┌─BUBOOK         ▲√ ansi     .sys     9,865  18/03/93   6:00  ...a ▲│
│  │▶DOS              √ append   .exe    10,774  18/03/93   6:00  ...a │
│  ├─HSG        ▸      √ atdosxl .sys    22,573  19/09/90  10:51  ...a │
│  ├─LLPRO            √ attrib   .exe    11,165  18/03/93   6:00  ...a │
│  ├─NAV             √ autoexec.bat        379   3/18/93  11:28  ...a │
│  ├─NORTON          √ autoexec.umb        378   3/18/93  12:03  ...a │
│  ├─ORGANIZE        √ bookdir  .set     4,486   7/18/93   9:26  ...a │
│  │ ├─ORGFILES      √ bookdsks.cat        66    7/18/93   9:36  ...a │
│  │ └─SAMPLE        √ bookdsks.set     4,486    7/18/93   9:33  ...a │
│  ├─PICS            √ chkdsk   .exe    12,907  18/03/93   6:00  ...a │
│  └─PSPRO          ▼√ chkstate.sys    41,600  18/03/93   6:00  ...a ▼│
│                                                                   │
│ Total Files:  1,625 [   69,403 K]  Selected Files:   147 [   5,766 K]│
│ ┌ Include ┐ ┌ Exclude ┐ ┌ Special ┐ ┌ Display ┐▸ ┌ OK ◂┐ ┌ Cancel ┐│
│                                                                   │
│ Select entire directories with right mouse button or Spacebar    │
└─────────────────────────────────────────────────────────────────┘
```

Move down the directory tree until your DOS directory is highlighted and then select all the files in that directory by clicking the right mouse button, or by pressing the space bar. Before leaving this option press **F1** and page through the help information on making selections. To allow you to be very specific about the type and properties of files selected for backup you could also experiment with the **Include**, **Exclude**, **Special** and **Display** selection buttons, which are located along the bottom of the box. To select directories and files from other drives to include in the backup you would click the drive letter at the top of the screen.

In this way you would build up a list of all the files on your system that you want to backup. In our example we will only select the DOS directory files, as this should be the same for most users. Press **OK** to leave the file selection box.

Click the **Options** button to change any settings like verification, compression, etc., as shown below.

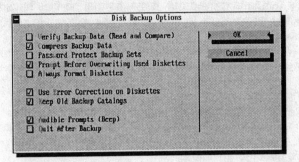

Use the **Backup Type** drop-down list box to select one of the three backup types available.

Full   backs up all selected files, regardless of whether or not they have changed since the last backup, and lowers the archive flags.

Incremental backs up all selected files that have changed since the last full or incremental backup, and lowers the archive flags. This type is for the partial backups in your backup cycle, if you work with different files each day. With this method it is important to save all incremental backup sets between full backups.

Differential backs up all selected files that have changed since the last full backup, but does not lower the archive flags. Since the archive flag is not lowered, the backed-up files will be backed up again in the next differential backup. Use this backup type if you generally work with the same files each day.

We will leave the **Full** option selected. Make sure the **Backup To** drop-down list box indicates your A: floppy drive as the destination for the backup files. Check the estimated number of disks and space required and make sure you have

131

that number of labelled disks ready. At long last we are ready to click the **S̲tart Backup** button to begin making the backup. If this button is greyed out, it means that no files have been selected for back up. In which case check your file selections and backup type.

All that remains now is to feed discs into your drive when they are requested. If you try to overwrite a previous backup disc, MSBACKUP will stop and give you the choice of changing the disc or overwriting the previous backup. Make sure you number the discs as they are used!

In our case four 1.44MB discs were needed (though only just), at a compression ratio of 1.4:1 and the procedure took a little over four minutes.

Saving a Setup File:

The backup we just carried out took four minutes to carry out, but probably a lot longer to set-up. However once you have set-up a backup procedure you can save the details, so that they are immediately available the next time you carry out a similar routine.

From the MSBACKUP main screen, select the menu option **F̲ile**, **Save Setup A̲s**, type 'DOSDIR' in the **File N̲ame** box and press <Enter> to save your settings. At any time in the future you can open this set-up from the **F̲ile** sub-menu. Press **Q** to return to DOS when you are ready.

Backup Catalogue Files:

As part of the backup process, MSBACKUP creates a backup catalogue (or catalog as used in the program) that contains information about the files you backed up. When you back up files, MSBACKUP places one copy of the backup catalogue on your hard disk, and a second copy on the disk or network drive that contains your backup set. When you need to restore any of the files, you can load the backup catalogue and easily select them from a backup set. A catalogue includes information about the original directory structure, the names, sizes, and attributes of the directories and files that were selected, the total number of files, the total size of the backup, the name of the set-up file that was used and the date the backup was made.

Each catalogue file is given a unique name that helps you identify a backup set, as shown in the Help window copied below.

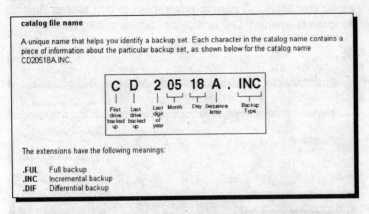

catalog file name

A unique name that helps you identify a backup set. Each character in the catalog name contains a piece of information about the particular backup set, as shown below for the catalog name CD20518A.INC.

C D 2 05 18 A . INC

First drive backed up
Last drive backed up
Last digit of year
Month
Day
Sequence letter
Backup Type

The extensions have the following meanings:

.FUL   Full backup
.INC   Incremental backup
.DIF   Differential backup

You should be able to easily locate the catalogue for a backup set from its filename, even with many catalogue files in your directory.

Each time you perform a full backup, using a specific set-up file, MSBACKUP creates a master catalogue. This master catalogue keeps track of all the other backup catalogues made during the rest of the backup cycle. When the next full backup is performed, a new backup cycle begins, and a new master catalogue is created.

The master catalogue is used if you need to restore a complete backup cycle. When you load the master catalogue, the catalogues of all the backups that were created during that backup cycle are automatically merged. This way the latest version of each backed-up file can be automatically restored.

Restoring a Backup:
The operation of restoring your files and directory structure is very similar to that described for backing them up originally. Now you have a set-up file, as long as you can remember it, you can force it to load by typing it on the command line when you enter the program, as follows:

```
msbackup dosdir
```

Select **Restore** from the opening dialogue box. If you did not specify a set-up file the DEFAULT.SET will be used and you will have to load the DOSDIR.SET with the **File**, **Open Setup** menu bar option. A control box similar to that for the Backup function is opened. Our completed box is shown below.

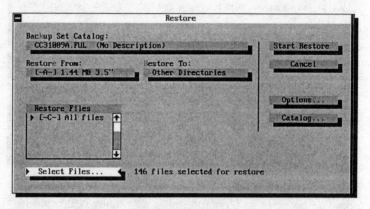

First make sure the **Restore From** box has your A: drive selected. Use the **Select Files** button to open the tree and file list screen and select the DOS directory, by right clicking it with your mouse, as described previously.

Restore To gives you three options for the destination of your restored files.

Original Locations - Restores your files to the drives and directories from which they were backed up.

Alternate Drives - Restores your files to a different drive. You are asked for the drive and path during the restore, before files backed up from each drive are restored. The files will be restored using the original directory structure under the path you specify.

Alternate Directories - Restores your files to different directories. You are asked for the directory names during the Restore process, before files backed up from each directory are restored.

For this exercise you should use the Alternate Directories option, as you do not want to overwrite all the files in your DOS directory.

If the original backup was carried out on another computer there would not be a copy of the catalogue file available on any of the hard drives of your current machine. In this case, to restore the files, you would need to copy the catalogue from the last floppy disc of the backup set. To do this press the **Catalog** button which opens the box shown below:

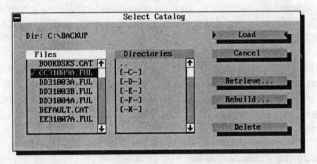

To load a catalogue from a floppy disc, put the last disc of the backup set into the A: drive and press the **Retrieve** button. Select the A: drive, select the required catalogue in the **F**iles list box and press the **L**oad button.

When all is complete, press the **Start Restore** button. The first of two 'Alert' boxes asks you to place the first backup disc into drive A:. The next box asks for the path to restore to; in our case we suggest C:\BUTRIAL, or something equally unlikely, which you can delete afterwards. At this stage we always lose our mouse, so you may have to use the <Tab> key to select the **C**ontinue button.

As with the backup operation, feed in the discs asked for without waiting for the drive to stop. That is what it expects! As the restore continues there are plenty of numbers being updated for you to watch. The lower right of the screen gives information on the current catalogue, and the left side shows details of the restore operation.

When the restoration is complete a detailed report is screened confirming that all is well and that, in our case, 146 files, with 5,904,877 bytes were restored in 3.07 minutes with no errors. Press **OK** followed by **Q** to return to DOS. Your mouse should have been restored as well. Unless you want two directories containing the same DOS files we suggest you delete the newly restored one, to save disc space.

A Backup Strategy:

Hopefully you should by now be completely sold on the MSBACKUP program we have been using. It is only any use though if you use it systematically and with discipline.

If you dig deeply in the Help files you will find much information on how to organise your backups. We suggest the following procedure may be useful to you if you generally work with different files each day. Set your partial backup type to **Incremental**. An incremental backup is also ideal where new files are created each day.

You have to keep the full backup set with all incremental backup sets. This is important since each incremental backup records a different increment of changes. The master catalogue will keep track of the full backup and all the subsequent incremental backups.

To use the incremental backup procedure:

1   In the **B_ackup To** drop-down list box, select MS-DOS Path and specify the path as A: or B:, depending on which drive you will use.

2   Perform a full backup of all your data files.

3   Each day, before you switch off, perform an incremental backup. Use the same floppy disk until it fills up, then start another disk.

4   Save all your floppy disks from the cycle until after you have performed the next full backup.

5   Perform the next full backup, maybe after one or two weeks, using different disks.

6   Perform the daily incremental backups as in step 3, and repeat the cycle.

It is also important to look after your backup disc sets. Label them carefully and write the catalogue name on them all. Also make sure you keep each complete set together, and if your data is very important, keep the backup sets well away from the computer.

With a little bit of discipline and a lot of MSBACKUP you should never have serious data loss problems, even if your hard disc explodes, or someone takes a liking to your computer.

File Recovery

We have all been in the position of desperately needing one of the files we deleted earlier in the day! With DOS 6, that need no longer be a problem. The UNDELETE utility provides three levels of protection for recovering previously deleted files.

Every disc in a DOS system has a File Allocation Table (FAT) and a Directory Table which hold the details of all the files stored on that disc. When a file is deleted, DOS sets its codes in the FAT to zero and replaces the first character of the file name in the directory table. This indicates that the space on the disc occupied by the file is available for use. At this stage the file itself is not removed from the disc.

Undelete:

The lowest level of recovery uses the 'MS-DOS Directory Method'. You don't do anything in advance with this method. When you want to recover a file, or files, that have been deleted, your chances of success depend on whether you have saved other files to the same area of the disc. If the original disc entries are not overwritten you should be able to recover previously deleted files.

The procedure is to type the command **UNDELETE** at the DOS prompt. The following is a typical session:

```
UNDELETE - A delete protection facility
Copyright (C) 1987-1993 Central Point Software, Inc.
All rights reserved.
Directory: D:\BOOK
File Specifications: *.*
    Delete Sentry control file not found.
    Deletion-tracking file not found.
    MS-DOS directory contains    6 deleted files.
    Of those,    6 files may be recovered.
Using the MS-DOS directory method.
    ?RED   SAM   58993 30/07/93 16:22 ...A  Undelete (Y/N)?n
    ?UINFO SAM    4504 10/10/93  8:32 ...A  Undelete (Y/N)?y
Please type the first character for ?UINFO  .SAM: b
File successfully undeleted.
```

In this case 6 deleted files in the current directory had not been overwritten and were easily recovered. In each case a prompt was made for the first character of the name.

The second level of protection is **Delete Tracking**. This requires you to place the following command line in your AUTOEXEC.BAT file

```
undelete /t
```

This opens a memory resident program which monitors the addresses of the clusters used by any files that are deleted, as well as the full file name. The information is stored in the file PCTRACKR.DEL.

When you use the Undelete command with tracking active, you have far more chance of recovering partially overwritten files.

The highest level of protection is known as **Delete Sentry.** This also requires you to place a command line in your AUTOEXEC.BAT file

```
undelete /s
```

This opens a memory resident program which actually moves the contents of deleted files to a hidden directory (Sentry). The file contents are kept there for seven days and then flushed out. If Sentry is active and the files are still stored, a successful recovery is almost inevitable.

At any time you can only have one of the two programs resident in memory, so if you are careless with your files you should decide which to use. Sentry gives the best protection, but can use enormous amounts of your hard disc, if you delete a lot of files (up to 20% by default).

Microsoft Anti-Virus

There has been much fuss in the press over the last few years about computer viruses. Programs and routines that are written with malicious intent and copy themselves from machine to machine, either from floppy discs or down a network or phone line. In fact they are not as common as some in the industry would have us believe, but it is well worth taking precautions against them.

DOS 6 includes an anti-virus program provided by Central Point Software. It seems powerful and has a very attractive graphical interface, which is accessed by typing **MSAV** at the DOS prompt. A screen similar to the one below should open.

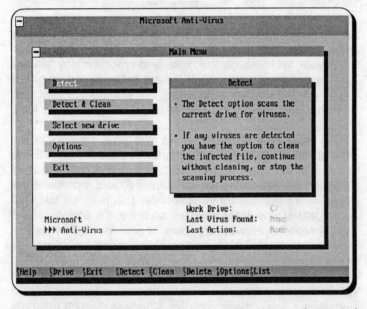

This is the control panel for the virus scanning package and has the following options:

Detect   Scans the current drive for viruses. If any viruses are detected you have the option to clean the infected file, continue without cleaning, or stop the scanning process.

Detect & Clean	Also scans the current drive for viruses. If a virus is detected, the infected file is cleaned and the scan continues to the next file.
Select new drive	This option displays the drive line, at the top of the screen, to enable you to select a different drive to scan and/or clean.
Options	Displays a dialogue box which allows you to Configure the program. Option settings can be saved when exiting from the program.

Simply select the drive you want to scan with the **Select new drive** option and press **Detect**. The program scans all the directories and files on the drive and reports if any viruses have been found. If you select **Detect & Clean** any viruses, if found, will be suitably disinfected. We will leave it to you to find your way around the rest of this package, as it is fairly intuitive.

The other part of MS-DOS 6's anti-virus armoury is the **VSAFE** memory resident program. You place the VSAFE command in your AUTOEXEC.BAT file (including any switches you need, see list in Chapter 8) and it continuously scans your computer for virus activity. This program takes up over 20KB of your RAM memory, so there is a downside. Our experience of such memory resident anti-virus utilities is that they get in the way of your day to day working and eventually you end up throwing them off the system.

Any anti-virus program is only as good as the information on viruses it contains. Such programs need continuous updates as new viruses and new strains of existing ones are found. Microsoft provide two vouchers in the back of the MS-DOS 6 update manual to enable you to get updates from Central Point. After that you must make your own arrangements to keep up to date.

8. MS-DOS COMMANDS

The following is a list of all the commands supported by the MS-DOS operating environment. The various commands are labelled internal or external, with external commands being accessible to the user only if the full filespec (drive and path) is given to where the appropriate command file resides. Examples of command usage is given whenever possible.

DOS 6 does not support the **assign.com**, **exe2bin.exe**, **graftabl.com**, and **join.exe** command files. These together with **4201.cpi**, **4208.cpi**, **5202.cpi**, **link.exe**, **msherc.com**, **printer.sys**, and **smartdrv.sys**, which are left behind in your DOS subdirectory when you upgrade from a previous version of DOS, can safely be deleted to free some 164KB of disc space.

Command	*Explanation*
append	External - sets a path that MS-DOS will search for data files when they are not in the current directory. It can EVEN be told not to search already defined paths.
	Example: append c:\wproc\docs
	searches the \wproc\docs directory on drive c: for data files.
	Switches:
	/e assigns the list of appended directories to an environment variable named APPEND. This switch can be used only the first time you use APPEND after starting your system. If you use /E, you can use the SET command to display the list of appended directories

/path:on	specifies whether a program is to search appended directories for a data file when a path is already included with the name of the file the program is looking for
/path:off	specifies that a program is not to search appended directories. The default setting is /path:on
/x:on	Specifies whether MS-DOS is to search appended directories when executing programs. You can abbreviate /x:on to /x. If you want to specify x:on, you must do it the first time you use APPEND after starting your system
/x:off	Specifies whether MS-DOS is not to search appended directories when executing programs. The default value is /x:off.

attrib [filespec]

External - sets or resets the *read only* attribute & archive bit of a file, and displays the attributes of a file.

Switches:
+a sets the archive bit of a file
−a clears the archive bit
+h sets the file as a hidden file
−h clears the hidden file attribute
+r sets read-only mode of a file
−r disables read-only mode.
+s sets the file as a system file
−s clears the system file attribute

	/s processes files in the current directory and all of its sub-directories.
	Example: attrib +r filespec
break	Internal - sets the Ctrl+Break or the extended Ctrl+C checking. This command can be used either at the command prompt or in the CONFIG.SYS file.
	Example: break ON
buffers	Internal - allocates memory for a specified number of disc buffers (1-99) from within your CONFIG.SYS file.
	Example: buffers=40,m
	where m is optional and specifies the number of the secondary buffer cache (0-8).
call	Internal - calls one batch file from another without exiting from the first one.
cd (or chdir)	Internal - changes the working directory to a different directory.
	Example: cd\wproc\docs
chcp [nnn]	Internal - selects current code page for as many devices as possible. Omitting *nnn* displays the current code page.
chkdsk [filespec]	External - has been replaced by **scandisk** in DOS 6.2. Chkdsk analyses the directories, files, and File Allocation Table (FAT) on the

logged or designated drive and produces a status report. It also reports the volume, serial number and disc allocation units.

Switches:
/f fixes any problems found during the check
/v causes the display of filespecs as they are being processed.

Example: chkdsk a:/f/v

choice

External - prompts the user to make a choice in a batch file.

Switches:
/c:keys specifies allowable keys in the prompt. When displayed, the keys will be followed by a question mark. If you don't specify the /c switch, choice uses YN as the default
/n causes choice not to display the prompt. The text before the prompt is still displayed, however. If you specify the /n switch, the specified keys are still valid
/s causes choice to be case sensitive
/t:c,nn causes choice to pause for a specified number of seconds nn (0-99), before defaulting to a specified key, shown above as switch c.

cls

Internal - clears the screen.

| command [filespec] | External - starts the command processor which is loaded into memory in two parts; the resident part and the transient part. If the transient part is overwritten by a program, it is reloaded. |

Switches:
/c executes a following command
/e specifies the environment size in bytes (160-32768, default = 160 bytes)
/k runs the specified program or batch file and then displays the DOS command prompt
/p prohibits command.com from exiting to a higher level.

Example:
command /c chkdsk a:

starts a new command processor under the current program, runs the chkdsk command on the disc in the A: drive, and returns to the first command processor.

| copy [filespec] | Internal - copies one or more files to specified disc. If preferred, copies can be given different names. |

Switches:
/a indicates an ASCII text file
/b indicates a binary file
/v causes the verification of data written on the destination disc.

Example: copy *.exe a:/v

copies all files with the .exe extension to the a: drive with verification.

145

country	External - enables DOS to use country-specific conventions for displaying dates, times, and currency. This command can only be used from within your CONFIG.SYS file.
ctty	Internal - changes the standard I/O console to an auxiliary (aux) console, and vice versa.

Example: ctty aux

moves all input/output from the current device (console) to an aux port such as another terminal.

The command *ctty con* moves I/O back to the console.

Valid values for the device parameter are prn, lpt1, lpt2, lpt3, con, aux, com1, com2, com3, and com4.

date	Internal - enters or changes the current date.
dblspace	External - starts the DoubleSpace program to set-up or configure compressed drives. Don't use this command from within Windows.
debug	External - starts the debug program that allows you to create or edit executable files.
defrag	External - reorganises files on a disc to optimise performance. Do not use this command from within Windows. Use the command by itself to open up a front-end, or with the following switches.

Switches:

/b	restarts your computer after files have been reorganised
/bw	starts program using a black and white colour system
/f	defragments files and ensures that the disk contains no empty spaces between files
/g0	disables the graphic mouse and graphic character set
/h	moves hidden files
/lcd	starts program using an lcd colour system
/u	defragments files and leaves empty spaces, if any, between files
/skiphigh	loads program into conventional memory. By default, it is loaded into upper memory, if available
/s	controls how the files are sorted in their directories. If you omit this switch, it uses the current order on the disk. The following list describes each of the values you can use to sort files. Use any combination of the values, and do not separate these values with spaces

	d	by date and time, earliest first
	d–	by date and time, latest first
	e	in alphabetic order by extension
	e–	in reverse alphabetic order by extension
	n	in alphabetic order by name
	n–	in reverse alphabetic order by name
	s	by size, smallest first
	s–	by size, largest first.

del [filespec]

Internal - deletes all files with the designated filespec.

Switch:
/p displays filenames to confirm deletion.

Example: del a:*.txt
deletes all .txt files from the a: drive.

deltree

External - deletes a specified directory and all the files and sub-directories that might be in it.

Switch:
/y carries out the command without first prompting you for confirmation.

device

Internal - loads a specified device driver into memory from within your CONFIG.SYS file.

devicehigh

External - loads a specified device driver into upper memory from within your CONFIG.SYS file.

| dir [filespec] | Internal - lists the files in a directory. |

Switches:

/a displays only the names of those directories and files with the attributes you specify. For example,

  a backup files
 -a files not changed since last backup
  d directory
 -d files only (not directories)
  h hidden files
 -h not hidden files
  r read-only files
 -r files other than read-only
  s system files
 -s non-system files.

/b lists each directory name or file, one per line (including the file extension)

/c displays information about file-compression ratios on Double Space drives

/l displays unsorted directory and filenames in lower case

/o: controls the sort order in which a directory listing is displayed. For example,

  c by compression ratio (lowest first)
 -c by compression ratio (highest first)
  d by date & time, earliest first
 -d by date & time, latest first
  e in alphabetical order by extension
 -e in reverse alphabetical order by extension

	g	with directories grouped before files
	−g	with directories grouped after files
	n	in alphabetical order
	−n	in reverse alphabetical order
	s	by size, smallest first
	−s	by size, largest first.

/p displays the directory listing a page at a time

/s lists every occurrence, in the specified directory and all sub-directories, of the specified filename

/w displays the directory listing in wide format.

diskcomp	External - compares the contents of the disc in the source drive to the disc in the destination drive.
diskcopy	External - copies the contents of the disc in the source drive to the disc in the destination drive

Switches:

/v verifies correct copying

/m forces multi-pass copy using memory only.

dos	Internal - specifies that DOS should maintain a link to the upper memory area, load part of itself into high memory area (HMA), or both. This command can only be used from within your CONFIG.SYS file.
doskey	External - starts the doskey program which recalls MS-DOS commands.

Switches:

/bufsize=   allows the specification of the buffer size to be used for storing commands. The default size is 512 bytes, while the minimum buffer size is 256 bytes

/insert   switches on the 'insert' mode

/history   displays a list of all commands stored in memory. The switch can be used with the re-direction symbol (>) to redirect the list to a file

/macros   displays a list of all doskey macros. The switch can be used with the re-direction symbol (>) to redirect the list to a file

/overstrike   switches on the 'overstrike' mode

/reinstall   installs a new copy of doskey and clears the buffer of the current copy.

dosshell   External - activates the front-end graphical interface (not distributed with version 6.2).

drivparm   External - allows you to define parameters for devices such as disc and tape drives when you start your computer. This command can only be used from within your CONFIG.SYS file.

echo	Internal - sets Echo to on or off.
edit	External - activates the MS-DOS screen editor which is used to create or edit ASCII text files.

Switches:
/b displays the editor in black and white
/g uses the fastest screen updating for CGA displays
/h displays the maximum number of lines possible for the monitor you are using.

emm386	External - enables or disables expanded memory support on a computer with an 80386 or higher processor.
erase	Internal - see del command.
exit	Internal - exits the command processor and returns to a previous level.
expand	External - expands a compressed file from a system disc.
fasthelp	External - provides a short summary of DOS 6 commands.
fastopen [filespec]	External - store in memory the location of directories and recently opened files on a specified drive.

Switch:
/x allows use of expanded memory. If this switch is used, then the **/x** switch must also be used with the **buffers** command.

fc [filespec]	External - compares two files and displays the differences between them.
	Switches:
	/a abbreviates the output of an ASCII comparison to only the first and last line of each set of differences
	/b compares binary files
	/c ignores the case of letters
	/l compares ASCII files line by line
	/n displays the line numbers during an ASCII comparison
	/t does not expand tabs to spaces
	/w compresses tabs and spaces during the comparison.
fcbs	Internal - specifies the number of file control blocks (FCBs) that DOS can have open at the same time (1-255, default = 4). This command can only be used from within your CONFIG.SYS file.
fdisk	External - sets up and partitions the fixed disc for use with DOS and other operating systems. It is also used to display and change the current active partition. The command supports an 80-column screen. It also has improved user-friendly commands to allow disc partitioning in megabytes or percentages instead of cylinders.
	Switch:
	/status displays an overview of the partition information without starting Fdisk.

files	Internal - specifies the number of files that DOS can access at one time. This command can only be used from within your CONFIG.SYS file.
find [filespec]	External - searches for a specific string of text in a specified ASCII file or files.

find [filespec]

Switches:
/c prints the count of lines containing the string
/i search is insensitive to the case of letters
/n precedes each occurrence with the relative line number in the file
/v displays all lines not containing the specified string.

Example: find "lost words" chap1 searches for the string *lost words* (which must appear within full quotes) in the named file (chap1).

for

Internal - repeats a command for each item in a set. This command can only be used at the command prompt or from within a batch file.

format [filespec]

External - formats the disc in the specified drive.

Switches:
/4 formats a double-sided disc with 40 tracks, 9 sectors per track for 360 KB in a high capacity (1.2 MB) disc drive per track
/8 formats with 8 sectors per track

/b   reserves space for the system
     files

/f:*size*

     specifies the size of the disc to
     be formatted. Use one of the
     following values for size, which
     specifies the capacity of the
     disc in Kbytes:

     160 / 180 for single-sided,
     double-density 5¼" discs,
     320 / 360 for double-sided,
     double-density 5¼" discs,
     720 for double-sided, double-
     density 3½" discs,
     1200 for double-sided, high-
     capacity 5¼" discs,
     1440 for double-sided, high-
     capacity 3½" discs,
     2880 for 2.88 MB, double-
     sided, 3½" discs.

/n   specifies the number of sectors
     per track, i.e. /n:9 for nine
     sectors
/q   deletes the file allocation table
     (FAT) and the root directory of
     a previously formatted disc
/s   copies the system files from
     the logged drive
/t   specifies the number of tracks,
     i.e. /t:40 for forty tracks
/v:label

     allows you to specify *label* with-
     out prompting after the format-
     ting process.

     Example: format a:/4/s

goto   Internal - jumps to a labelled line
            within the same batch file.

graphics	External - it supports EGA and VGA graphics modes to provide screen dumps to IBM Graphics, Proprinters and compatibles.

Switches:
/b   prints the background in colour
/lcd prints an image by using the liquid crystal display aspect ratio instead of the CGA aspect ratio
/r   prints the image as it appears on the screen (white characters on a black background, rather than reversed). |
| help | External - provides online information about the MS-DOS commands.

Switches:
/b   allows use of monochrome monitor with a colour graphics card
/g   provides fast update of a CGA screen
/h   displays maximum number of lines possible with your hardware
/nohi allows use of monitor that does not support high intensity. |
| if | Allows conditional execution of commands within a batch file. |
| include | Internal - includes the contents of one configuration block within another. This command can only be used from within your CONFIG.SYS file. |

install	Internal - loads a memory-resident program into memory. This command can only be used from within your CONFIG.SYS file.
interlnk	External - starts the Interlnk program, which connects two computers via their parallel or serial ports and enables them to share discs and printer ports.
intersvr	External - starts the Interlnk server.
keyb [xx]	External - selects a special keyboard layout. Omitting **xx** returns the current status of the keyboard. Switches: /e specifies that an enhanced keyboard is installed /id: specifies the keyboard in use.
label	External - creates or changes the volume identification label on a disc.
lastdrive	Internal - specifies the maximum number of drives you can access. This command can only be used from within your CONFIG.SYS file.
loadfix	External - forces programs to load above the first 64 KB of conventional memory.
loadhigh (lh)	Internal - loads a program into the upper memory area.
md (or mkdir)	Internal - creates a new directory on the specified disc.

| mem | External - it reports the amounts of conventional, expanded and extended memory that are available. |

Switches:

/c	displays the status of programs loaded in conventional and upper memory area
/d	displays the status of currently loaded programs and of internal drivers
/free	lists the free areas of conventional and upper memory
/module	shows how a program module is currently using memory
/page	pages screen output. Can be used with all the other switches.

| memmaker | External - starts the MemMaker program, which optimises your computer's memory by configuring device drivers and memory resident programs to run in the upper memory area. Don't use this program from within Windows. |

Switches:

/b	displays MemMaker in black and white
/batch	forces it to take all the default options
/session	used by MemMaker during memory optimisation
/swap:drive	specifies the letter of the original start-up drive

/t	disables the detection of Token Ring networks
/undo	forces MemMaker to undo the most recent changes
/w:s1,s2	specifies the amount of upper memory space for Windows translation buffers.

menucolor	External - sets the text and background colours for the startup menu. This command can only be used from within a menu block in your CONFIG.SYS file.
menudefault	External - specifies the default menu item on the startup menu and sets a time-out value, if desired. This command can only be used from within a menu block in your CONFIG.SYS file.
menuitem	External - defines up to nine items on the startup menu. This command can only be used from within a menu block in your CONFIG.SYS file.
mode [options]	External - sets the mode of operation on a display monitor, parallel/serial printer or the RS232C port. The keyboard repetition and auto-repeat start delay time can be set. Also, it allows the setting of the number of rows to any of 25, 43 or 50 on the screen, and there is a wider range of serial-port configurations.

Options:

Display: mode [n]

40	sets display width to 40 characters per line
80	sets display width to 80 characters per line
bw40	sets screen to black and white display with 40 characters
bw80	sets screen to black and white display with 80 characters
co40	sets screen to colour display with 40 characters
co80	sets screen to colour display with 80 characters
mono	sets screen to monochrome with 80 characters.

Printer: mode LPTi: [n][,[m][,p]]

i	sets printer number with legal values from 1 to 3
n	sets number of characters per line with legal values of 80 or 132
m	sets the number of lines per inch with legal values of 6 or 8
p	allows continuous re-entry on a time-out error.

Example: mode LPT1: 132,8

sets the printer in the first parallel port to 132 characters per line and 8 lines per inch.

Serial printer: mode LPTi:=COMj
It redirects all output sent to one of the parallel printer ports to one of the serial (RS232C) ports.

Before using this command, the serial port must be initialized using the *p* switch of the printer mode command.

i   sets printer number with legal values from 1 to 3
j   sets the serial port with legal values of 1 or 2.

more
External - sends output to the console one screen-full at a time.

Example: type read.me | more

displays the contents of the read.me file one screen at a time.

move
External - moves one or more files to the specified location. It can also be used to rename files and directories.

msav
External - starts the Anti-Virus program, which scans your computer for known viruses.

Switches:
/a scans all drives except drive A: and B:
/c scans and removes viruses from specified drive
/l scans all local drives except network drives
/n lists contents of MSAV file
/r reports and lists files checked in MSAV file
/s scans specified drive but does not remove viruses.

Several other switches exist which control your hardware. To find out more about these, use Help.

msbackup	External - starts the Backup program, which backs up or restores one or more files from one disc onto another.
mscdex	External - provides access to CD-ROM drives.
msd	External - starts the Diagnostics program, which provides technical information on your computer.
nlsfunc	External - provides support for extended country information and allows the use of **chcp** command to select code pages for all devices defined as having code page switching support.
numlock	Internal - specifies whether the NUMLOCK key is set ON or OFF. This command can only be used from within your CONFIG.SYS file.
path	Internal - sets and displays the path to be searched by DOS for external commands or batch files. Example: path c:\;c:\dos;c:\comms will search the root directory as well as the dos and comms sub-directories for files with .COM, .EXE, and .BAT extensions.
pause	Internal - suspends processing of a batch file and displays a message that prompts you to press any key to continue.
power	External - turns power management on or off, reports the status

of power management, and sets levels of power conservation.

print [filespec]

External - can be used to print text files in background mode, while other tasks are being performed. Using the command without options displays files already in the print queue.

Switches:
/b sets size of internal buffer with legal values from 512 to 16384 bytes, speeding up printing
/c allows cancellation of files in the print queue. It can be used with the /p switch
/d specifies the print device such as PRN or AUX
/p allows the addition of files to the print queue. Both /c & /p can be used in the same command line
/q specifies the number of files in the print queue, normally 10, with legal values from 4 to 32
/t allows cancellation of files in print queue.

prompt

Internal - changes the command prompt.

Example: pg

which allows the path of the current working directory to be displayed as the prompt.

qbasic

External - activates the MS-DOS QBasic program that reads instructions written in the Basic computer language.

163

Switches:

/b	displays QBasic in black and white
/editor	activates the MS-DOS screen editor
/g	provides the fastest update of a CGA monitor
/h	displays the maximum number of display lines possible for the type of monitor used
/nohi	allows use of a monitor that does not support high intensity
/run	runs the specified Basic program before displaying it.

rd (or rmdir)   Internal - removes the specified directory.

rem   Enables you to include comments in batch files.

ren (or rename)   Internal - changes the file name.

Example: ren a:\doc\mem1 mem2

will rename the mem1 file, which is to be found in sub-directory doc on a disc in the a: drive, to mem2.

replace [options]   External - allows easy updating of files from a source disc to a target disc of files having the same name.

Switches:
/a adds new files that exist on the source disc but not on the target disc. This switch can not be used with the /s or /u switch

	/p prompts the user before replacing
	/r replaces read only files, as well as unprotected files
	/s searches all subdirectories of the destination directory and replaces matching files. You can not use the /s switch with the /a switch
	/u updates files with a time and date on the source disc more recent than those on the destination disc. You can not use the /u switch with the /a switch
	/w waits for you to insert a disc before replace begins to search for source files.
restore [options]	External - restores one or more files that were backed up using the *backup* command of DOS versions 2.0 - 5.0. This command is NOT used for DOS version 6 backup files.

Switches:
/a:date or /b:date
    restores those files last modified on or before the specified date. The date format varies according to the country setting in your CONFIG.SYS file
/d displays a list of the files on the backup disc that match the names specified in *filename* without restoring any files
/e:time or /l:time
    restores only those files last modified on or before the specified time (according to the country setting)

	/m restores only those files modified since the last backup
	/n restores only those files that no longer exist on the destination disc
	/p prompts user before overwriting an existing file by restoring
	/s restores files in the specified directory and all files in any sub-directories of the specified directory.
scandisk	External - scans and repairs specified discs.

Switches:
/all checks and repairs all local drives
/autofix fixes damage without prompting you first. By default, if you start Scan-Disk with this switch and it finds lost clusters on your drive, it saves the lost clusters as files in the drive's root directory
/checkonly
checks a drive for errors, but does not repair any damage. You cannot use this switch with the /auto-fix or /custom switches
/custom runs ScanDisk using the configuration settings in the [Custom] section of the SCANDISK.INI file. The switch is useful for running ScanDisk from a batch program. It can't be used with the /autofix or /checkonly switches |

/mono	configures ScanDisk to use a monochrome display. Instead of specifying this switch every time you run ScanDisk, include the 'display=mono' line in your SCANDISK.INI file
/nosave	directs ScanDisk to delete any lost clusters it finds. Can be used only with the /autofix switch
/nosummary	
	prevents ScanDisk from displaying a full-screen summary after checking each drive
/surface	automatically performs a surface scan after checking other areas of a drive. During a surface scan of an uncompressed drive, it confirms that data can be reliably written and read from the scanned drive. During a surface scan of a DoubleSpace drive, it confirms that data can be decompressed.
set	Internal - sets strings into the command processor's environment. The general form of the command is:
	set [name=[parameter]]
	Set by itself displays the current environment.
setver	External - displays the version table.

share   External - installs file sharing and
                           locking.

                           Switches:
                           /f: allocates file space, in bytes.
                               The default value is 2048
                           /l: sets the number of files that
                               can be locked at one time. The
                               default is 20.

shell   Internal - specifies the name and
                           location of the command
                           interpreter you want DOS to use.
                           This command can only be used
                           from within your CONFIG.SYS file.

shift   Internal - allows more than 10
                           replaceable parameters in a batch
                           file.

smartdrv   External - creates a disc cache in
                           extended memory which speeds
                           up access to your hard disc. This
                           command can either be used at
                           the command prompt or from
                           within your AUTOEXEC.BAT file.

                           Parameters:
                           [[drive+|-] Specifies the letter of
                           the drive for caching control. The
                           plus (+) sign enables caching,
                           while the minus (–) sign disables it.
                           A drive letter without a plus or
                           minus sign, enables read-caching
                           and disables write-caching.

                           Switches:
                           /e:size specifies in bytes the
                                   'element' size of the cache
                                   that moves at a time.
                                   Valid values are 1024,
                                   2048, 4096, and 8192

(default=8192). The larger the size, the more conventional memory is used

/b:size   specifies the 'buffer' size in kilobytes of the read-ahead buffer - the additional data read from the hard disc by an application (default=16 K)

/c   writes all cached data from memory to disc - use this option if you are going to turn off your computer

/r   clears the contents of the existing cache and restarts SMARTDrive

/l   prevents SMARTDrive from automatically loading into upper memory blocks, even if these are available. You can use this switch if upper memory is enabled for use by programs

/q   stops status messages when SMARTDrive starts. This switch cannot be used with the /v switch

/v   enables SMARTDrive to display status and error messages when it starts. (By default, it does not display any messages unless it encounters an error condition.) This switch cannot be used with the /q switch

/s   displays additional information about SMARTDrive's status.

sort [filespec]	External - reads data from the console or a file, sorts it and sends it to the console or file.
	Switches:
	/r sorts in reverse order
	/+n sorts the file according to the character in column n.
	Example: dir | sort
	sorts the output of the *dir* command in alphabetical order.
stacks	Internal - supports the dynamic use of data stacks to handle hardware interrupts. Use only from within the CONFIG.SYS file.
submenu	Internal - defines an item on a startup menu that, when selected, displays another set of options. Use only from within the CONFIG.SYS file.
subst	External - allows substitution of a virtual drive for an existing drive and path.
	Switch:
	/d deletes a virtual drive.
	Example: subst d: a:\wproc\docs
	will cause future reference to drive d: to be taken as replacement to the longer reference to a:\wproc\docs.
switches	Internal - specifies from within your CONFIG.SYS file special DOS options.

Switches:

/f skips the 2-second delay after displaying the "Starting MS-DOS ..." message during start-up

/k forces an enhanced keyboard to behave like a conventional keyboard

/n prevents you from using the F5 or F8 key to bypass startup commands

/w specifies that the wina20.386 file has been moved to a directory other than the root directory.

sys   External - transfers the DOS system files from the logged drive to the disc in the specified drive. It also allows the specification of source drive and path commands to transfer system files across a network.

time   Internal - displays and sets the system time. It also supports a 12- or 24-hour format.

tree   External - displays the directory structure in graphical form.

Switches:

/a specifies that tree is to use text characters instead of graphic characters

/f displays the named of the files in each directory.

type   Internal - displays the contents of a file on the console.

undelete	External - restores files which were previously deleted with the del command.

Switches:

/all	recovers all deleted files without prompting
/dos	recovers only those files that are internally listed as deleted by MS-DOS, prompting for confirmation
/ds	recovers only those files listed in the SENTRY directory, prompting for confirmation on each file
/dt	recovers only the files listed in the deletion-tracking file
/list	lists deleted files that are available to be recovered
/load	loads the memory-resident portion of the Undelete program
/unload	removes the memory-resident portion of the Undelete program
/purge	deletes the contents of the SENTRY directory
/s	enables the Delete Sentry level of protection and loads the memory-resident portion of the UNDELETE program
/status	displays the type of delete protection in effect for each drive
/t	enables the Delete Tracker level of protection and loads the memory-resident portion of the UNDELETE program.

unformat	External - restores a disc erased by the format command or restructured by the recover command.

Switches:

/l	when used with the /partn switch, lists every file and subdirectory found by unformat
/p	sends output messages to the printer connected to LPT1
/test	shows how unformat will recreate the information of the disc.

ver	Internal - displays the PC/MS-DOS version number.
verify	Internal - allows the verify switch to be turned ON or OFF. Example: verify OFF
vol	Internal - displays the disc volume label, if it exists.
vsafe	External - monitors for viruses.
xcopy [filespec]	External - copies files and directories, including lower level sub-directories, if they exist, to the destination drive and directory.

Switches:

/a	copies source files that have their archive bit set
/d:	copies source files which were modified on or after a specified date
/e	copies sub-directories even if they are empty - use this switch in conjunction with /s

/m copies archived files only, but also turns off the archive bit in the source file

/p prompts the user with '(Y/N?)'

/s copies directories and their sub-directories unless they are empty

/v causes verification of each file as it is written

/w displays a message before starting to copy.

9. GLOSSARY OF TERMS

Application
Software (program) designed to carry out certain activity, such as word processing.

ASCII
It is a binary code representation of a character set. The name stands for 'American Standard Code for Information Interchange'.

AUTOEXEC.BAT
A batch file containing commands which are automatically executed on booting up the system.

BACKUP
To make a back-up copy of a file or a disc for safekeeping.

Base memory
The first 1 MB of random access memory.

BASIC
A high level programming language. The name stands for 'Beginner's All-purpose Symbolic Instruction Code'.

Batch file
An ASCII formatted file that contains MS-DOS commands which can be executed by the computer.

Baud
The unit of measurement used to describe data transmission speed. One baud is one bit per second.

BIOS
The Basic Input/Output System. It allows the core of the operating system to communicate with the hardware.

Bit	A binary digit; the smallest unit of information that can be stored, either as 1 or as 0.
Bitmap	A technique for managing the image displayed on a computer screen.
Boot	To start up the computer and load the DOS operating system.
Booting up	The process of starting up the computer.
Branching	Transferring execution of commands to another part of a batch file.
Buffer	RAM memory allocated to store data being read from disc.
Byte	A grouping of binary digits (0 or 1) which represent information.
Cache	An area of memory reserved for data, which speeds up access to a disc.
Card	A removable printed-circuit board that is plugged into an expansion slot.
CGA	Colour Graphics Adaptor; 2 modes and 4 colours - almost obsolete.
Cluster	A unit of one or more sectors. It is the minimum amount of space that can be allocated to a file on disc.
Click	To quickly press and release a mouse button.
Clipboard	An area of memory, also called a buffer, where text, graphics,

and commands can be stored to await further action.

Code page	A table in DOS that defines which extended ASCII character set is used in a document.
Cold boot	The process of starting your PC by turning on the power switch.
Command	An instruction given to a computer to carry out a particular action.
COMMAND.COM	The Operating System's Command Processor which analyses what is typed at the keyboard and causes execution of appropriate commands.
Command line	The line on the computer's screen into which you enter DOS commands.
Command Prompt	The prompt (C>) which appears on the computer's screen to let you know that MS-DOS is ready to receive a command.
CONFIG.SYS	A special file that allows the system to be configured closer to requirement.
Conventional Memory	The first 640 KB of base memory, used by DOS programs.
Coprocessor	A processor for doing specialist tasks, such as a maths coprocessor. It reduces the load on the CPU.
CPU	The Central Processing Unit; the main chip that executes all instructions entered into a computer.

Current directory	The directory that is searched first for a requested file.
Cursor	The blinking line indicating where the next input can be entered.
Default	The command, device or option automatically chosen by the system.
Device driver	A special file that must be loaded into memory for DOS to be able to address a specific procedure or hardware device. These are normally installed from the CONFIG.SYS file at system start-up.
Device name	A logical name used by DOS to identify a device, such as LPT1 or COM1 for the parallel or serial printer.
Dialogue box	A box that MS-DOS displays on the screen when DOSSHELL is in operation, to ask the user for more information.
Directory	An area on disc where information relating to a group of files is kept.
Directory identifier	Displays the active disc drive and directory on the File System screen of DOSSHELL.
Directory tree	A pictorial representation of your disc's structure.
Disc	A device on which you can store programs and data.

Disc file	A collection of program code, or data, that is stored under a given name on a disc.
DOS	The Disc Operating System. A collection of small specialised programs that allow interaction between user and computer.
DOS Extender	Software that allows DOS programs to run in extended memory.
DOS prompt	The prompt displayed on the screen, such as A> or C>, indicating that DOS is ready to accept commands when not working with DOSSHELL.
DOSSHELL	The name of the front-end graphical interface provided by MS-DOS 5.
Double-click	To quickly press and release a mouse button twice.
DPI	Dots Per Inch - a resolution standard for laser printers.
DR-DOS	Digital Research's (now owned by Novell) implementation of the Disc Operating System for compatible PCs.
Drag	To press and hold down the left mouse button while moving the mouse.
Drive name	The letter followed by a colon which identifies a floppy or hard disc drive.
Driver	A set of commands used to run a peripheral device (see device driver).

Edit	The MS-DOS screen editor which is used to create and modify ASCII formatted files, such as batch files, and the CONFIG.SYS file.
EGA	Enhanced Graphics Adaptor; it has 6 modes and 16 colours.
EISA	Extended Industry Standard Architecture, for construction of PCs with the Intel 32 bit microprocessor.
EMM	Expanded Memory Manager.
Enter key	The key that must be pressed after entering data.
EMS	The Expanded Memory Specification developed by Lotus, Intel and Microsoft to enable programs to use Expanded memory and provided in DOS 5 & 6 by EMM386.EXE.
Expanded memory	This is memory outside the conventional RAM (first 640 K) that DOS uses. It can be used by software to store data and run applications.
Extended memory	This is memory above the 1-MByte memory address which DOS can use for certain operations.
External command	A command DOS executes by first loading it from an external disc file.
FAT	The File Allocation Table. An area on disc where information is kept on which part of the disc the file is to be found.

File	The name given to an area on disc containing a program or data.
File extension	The optional three-letter suffix following the period in a filename.
File list	A list of filenames contained in the active directory.
Filename	The name given to a file. It must not exceed 8 characters in length and can have an extension of up to 3 characters.
Filespec	File specification made up of drive, path, filename and a three letter extension.
Fixed disc	The hard disc of a computer.
Floppy disc	A removable disc on which information can be stored magnetically. There are two types of floppy discs; a 5¼" flexible disc and a 3½" stiff disc.
Formatting	The process of preparing a disc so that it can store information. During formatting, sectors, tracks, a directory, and the FAT are created on the disc.
Function key	One of the series of 10 or 12 keys marked with the letter F and a numeral, used for specific operations.
Gigabyte	1,024 Megabytes.
Graphics card	A device that controls the display on the monitor and other allied functions.

GUI	A Graphical User Interface, such as that of DOSSHELL which uses visual displays to eliminate the need for typing commands.
Hardcopy	Output on paper.
Hard disc	A device built into the computer for holding programs and data. It is sometimes referred to as the fixed disc.
Hardware	The equipment that makes up a computer system, excluding the programs or software.
Help	A feature that gives you instructions and additional information on using DOS (DOS applications normally include their own help system).
Hidden files	Files that do not normally appear in a directory listing, such as the IO.SYS and MSDOS.SYS files.
Highlight	The change to a reverse-video appearance when a menu item or area of text is selected.
HIMEM.SYS	The system file that allows the use of extended memory by DOS programs.
HMA	High Memory Area; the first 64KB of memory beyond the end of the base memory, which DOS software can access.
Icon	A small graphic image that represents a function. Clicking on an icon produces an action.

Internal command	One of a set of many commands available to you at any time as they are loaded into memory every time you start your PC.
Interface	A device that allows you to connect a computer to its peripherals.
ISA	Industry Standard Architecture; a standard for internal connections in PCs.
Key combination	When two or more keys are pressed simultaneously, such as Ctrl+Alt+Del.
Kilobyte	(KB); 1024 bytes of information or storage space.
LABEL	The MS-DOS command which allows you to give a name to your disc.
LAN	Local Area Network; PCs, workstations or minis sharing files and peripherals within the same site.
LCD	Liquid Crystal Display.
Macro	A suite of programming commands invoked by one keystroke.
MCA	Micro Channel Architecture; IBM's standard for construction of PCs introduced in the 1990s.
Megabyte	(MB); 1024 kilobytes of information or storage space.
Megahertz	(MHz); Speed of processor in million of cycles per second.

Memory	Part of computer consisting of storage elements organised into addressable locations that can hold data and instructions.
Menu	A list of available options as appears in the DOSSHELL.
Menu bar	The horizontal bar that lists the names of menus.
Microprocessor	The calculating chip within a computer.
Minicomputer	A small mainframe computer to which terminals can be attached.
MIPS	Million Instructions Per Second; measures speed of a system.
Monitor	The display device connected to your PC.
Mouse	A device used to manipulate a pointer around your display and activate a certain process by pressing a button.
MS-DOS	Microsoft's implementation of the Disc Operating System for compatible PCs.
Network server	Central computer which stores files for several linked computers.
Operating System	A group of programs that translates your commands to the computer.
OS/2	An alternative operating system to DOS for powerful PCs, introduced in 1988.
Parallel interface	A device that allows transfer of blocks of data in bytes.

Parameter	Additional information appended to an MS-DOS command to indicate how the command should be executed.
PATH	The drive and directories that DOS should look in for files.
PC	Personal Computer.
PC-DOS	IBM's implementation of DOS for IBM PCs.
PCX	A standard file format used for bitmapped graphics.
Peripheral	Any device attached to a PC.
Pixel	A picture element on screen; the smallest element that can be indepenently assigned colour and intensity.
Port	An input/output address through which your PC interacts with external devices.
Print queue	The list of print jobs waiting to be sent to a printer.
Program	A set of instructions which cause the computer to perform certain tasks.
Prompt	The System prompt displayed on screen, such as A> or C>, indicating that DOS is ready to accept commands.
Protected mode	The operating mode of 286 (and higher) processors, not normally used by DOS. It allows more than 1 MB of memory to be addressed.

Protocol	It defines the way in which data is transferred between different hardware.
Processor	The electronic device which performs calculations.
PS/2	The range of PCs first introduced by IBM in late 1980s.
RAM	Random Access Memory. The micro's volatile memory. Data held in it is lost when power is switched off.
Real mode	The normal operating mode of PCs, in which only the first 1 MB of memory can be addressed.
Return key	The same as the Enter key.
ROM	Read Only Memory. The micro's non-volatile memory. Data are written into this memory at manufacture and are not affected by power loss.
Root directory	The main disc directory under which a number of subdirectories can be created.
Scroll bar	The bar that appears at the right side of the File List and Directory sections of the File System screen of DOSSHELL.
Sector	Disc space, normally 512 bytes long.
Serial interface	An interface that transfers data as individual bits; each operation has to be completed before the next starts.

SHELL	A front end to DOS or an alternative Command Processor.
Software	The programs and instructions that control your PC's functionality.
Spooler	Software which handles transfer of information to a store where it will be used by a peripheral device.
SVGA	Super Video Graphics Array; it has all the VGA modes but with 256 colours.
System	Short for computer system, implying a specific collection of hardware and software.
System disc	A disc containing DOS' three main files and other Utilities.
System prompt	The prompt displayed on the screen, such as A> or C> indicating that DOS is ready to accept commands when not working with DOSSHELL.
Text file	A file saved in ASCII format. It contains text characters, but no formatting codes.
Title bar	A horizontal bar across the top of each screen in DOSSHELL that contains the name of the screen.
Toggle	A term used to describe something that turns on and off with the same switch.
TSR	Terminate and Stay Resident programs, that is, memory resident programs.

UMB	A block of upper memory made available by a 386 memory manager into which memory resident software can be loaded.
Upper memory	The 384KB of memory between the top of conventional memory and the end of the base memory.
VGA	Video Graphics Array; has all modes of EGA, but with 16 colours.
Volume label	An identifying label written to a disc when a disc is first formatted.
Warm boot	The process of starting your PC with the use of the Ctrl+Alt+Del key combination.
Wildcard character	A character that can be included in a filename to indicate any character (?) or group of characters (*) that might match that position in other filenames.
Windows	A program developed by Microsoft in which applications can appear in graphical form.
XMS	The Extended Memory Specification developed by Microsoft to allow DOS programs to use extended memory. This is provided in DOS 5 & 6 by HIMEM.SYS.

INDEX

COMPANION DISC TO THIS BOOK

This book contains many pages of file/program listings. There is no reason why you should spend hours typing them into your computer, unless you wish to do so, or need the practice.

The COMPANION DISC for this book comes with all the example listings. It is available in both 3.5-inch and 5.25-inch formats.

COMPANION DISCS for all books written by the same author(s) and published by BERNARD BABANI (publishing), are also available and are listed at the front of this book. Make sure you specify the BP book number and the book title in your order.

ORDERING INSTRUCTIONS

To obtain your copy of the companion disc, fill-in the order form below, enclose a cheque (payable to **P.R.M. Oliver**) or a postal order, and send it to the address given below.

Book No.	Book Name	Unit Price	Total Price
BP ___		£3.50	
BP ___		£3.50	
BP ___		£3.50	
Name .... Address		Sub-total	£..............
		P & P (@ 45p/disc)	£..............
Disc Format 3.5-inch....... 5.25-inch.......		Total Due	£..............
Send to: P.R.M. Oliver, CSM, Pool, Redruth, Cornwall, TR15 3SE			

PLEASE NOTE

The author(s) are fully responsible for providing this Companion Disc service. The publishers of this book accept no responsibility for the supply, quality, or magnetic contents of the disc, or in respect of any damage, or injury that might be suffered or caused by its use.